V O L U M E   O N E

Treasured
MENNONITE
RECIPES

Recipes from Mennonite Relief Sale Volunteers

Fox Chapel Publishing
Box 7948M
Lancaster, PA 17604
(717) 399-7999 Fax (717) 399-8102

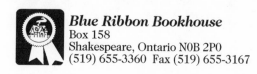
Blue Ribbon Bookhouse
Box 158
Shakespeare, Ontario N0B 2P0
(519) 655-3360 Fax (519) 655-3167

Treasured Mennonite Recipes is published by
Fox Chapel Publishing— a for-profit publishing company. A portion of the proceeds from the
cookbook sales is donated to Mennonite Central Committee to support their work of worldwide
relief and development.

For further information on Mennonite Central Committee please write to the office nearest you.
North American offices are listed in the
"Directory of Relief Sales" in the back of this book.

Treasured Mennonite Recipes—Volume One,
is the first titles in a new series.
Volume Two—containing all new recipes plus photos and
personal anecdotes—will be available in 1993.

USA ISBN# 1-56523-025-6
1992 by Fox Chapel Publishing Inc.
All Rights Reserved.

*To order copies of this book, please send cover price plus $2.00
postage. Please try your bookseller first.*

Published in Canada By:
Blue Ribbon Bookhouse
Box 158
Shakespeare, Ontario N0B 2P0
Phone (519)655-3360 Fax (519)655-3167
Canadian ISBN# 1-895363-12-8

Cover illustrations painted by Pam McKee/Inklinations, Romanville, PA.

Interior Design and Layout by The Reese Group, Ephrata, PA.
Cover Text and Design by Hamilton Design, Lancaster, PA.
Manufactured in the United States of America.

Table of Contents

Publisher's Foreword i

Who Are the Mennonites? iii

History of the Relief Sales vi

Breads

    Yeast 1–8

    Quick 9–22

Cakes and Frostings 23–36

Candies 37–42

Cookies, Squares and Bar Cookies 43–66

Casseroles and Supper Dishes 67–82

    Main Dishes 83–94

Desserts 95–110

Pies and Tarts 111–124

Pickles and Relishes 125–134

Punches and Drinks 135–144

Salads and Salad Dressings 145–158

Soups 159–164

Special European Mennonite Dishes 165–178

Traditional Classics—Recipes and Menus 179–188

Grandma's Remedies 189–195

Directory of Relief Sales/U.S.A. and Canada 197–200

Index 201–215

Order Form 216–219

Conversion Chart 220

Publisher's Foreword

If you've never been to a Mennonite Relief Sale, this book will give you a glimpse into the good food and fun you've been missing.

Relief sales are organized by local volunteers from the Mennonite and Brethren in Christ Churches. The purpose of the sales is to raise money for Third World development and relief projects. Because the sales are a grass-roots effort; the character of each sale is unique. Some sales are organized in the traditional Pennsylvania Dutch areas. Other sales are run by committees of church members from more diverse backgrounds.

This volume focuses on the more traditional cookery of the Swiss-German Mennonites.

Volume Two, due in 1993, will include recipes and traditions from all the different sales.

There are certain things you will find, whenever you visit a Relief Sale—good food, great bargains and a warm friendly atmosphere. You never know what will be donated for the auction—at a recent sale, you could place your bid on several live llamas!

You will enjoy the wonderful taste of these recipes gathered from Mennonite Relief Sale volunteers.

Who Are the Mennonites?

"For other foundation can no man lay than that is laid, which is Jesus Christ."

I Corinthians 3:11
(Menno Simons's favorite Biblical verse)

The religious family of faith that is today called Mennonite began in Switzerland in the sixteenth century during the religious upheaval of the Protestant Reformation. A small group of believers rejected the teachings of both Martin Luther and Ulrich Zwingli, two prominent Reformation leaders, as falling short of the Bible's instructions for a Christian life. This group, which began to meet secretly in the homes of its members, felt a return to the teachings of Jesus Christ as recorded in the New Testament was in order. Central to this movement were two beliefs: that a truly Christian religious community be made up of committed adult members who had voluntarily declared their faith (their adherence to the principles of Jesus's teachings) before baptism and that this Christian fellowship (or church) be free from state influence. In January 1525 members of this Swiss group, lead by Conrad Grebel, confessed their faith in Jesus Christ and baptised one another at Zurich, in defiance of the rules of the state.

Threatened by this movement, the official churches of the day opposed it, calling its followers Anabaptizers, or re-baptizers. Despite the Anabaptists' assertions that the Scriptures supported their position, neither the Roman church nor the Reformist groups would tolerate this deviation. Many early movement leaders met death at the hands of church-supported persecutors and thousands more followers would die over the next two generations.

Despite persecution, the Anabaptist movement spread to other countries, among them the Netherlands. There Menno Simons, a Catholic priest, began to question the doctrine of the mass and the practice of infant baptism. In 1536, after searching the Bible for answers to his doubts, he joined the Anabaptist movement. A tireless organizer of house-church groups, Simons provided a unifying force for the movement through preaching and extensive writings about the reforms. Others began to call his followers Menists (in English, Mennonite)—and later to apply the term to the entire Anabaptist movement. The group itself preferred to be known as Taufgesinnt, which in English means "those who baptize on confession of faith."

Migration—prompted by intolerance and persecution—was for centuries a way of life for many Mennonites. The first Mennonite community in North America was founded in 1683, in Pennsylvania, by German-speaking European immigrants. Later, descendants of this group moved to the western United States. In the nineteenth and twentieth centuries many Dutch and North German Mennonites traveled to Prussia (later Poland), South Russia, and then to the central United States and Canada in search of the freedom to practice their religious beliefs. Others settled in South America in the periods following World War I, the Russian Revolution, and World War II. Lancaster County, Pennsylvania, is today home to the largest Mennonite community in the world. The second largest is found in Winnipeg, Manitoba, Canada.

Today in 44 countries throughout the world—across Africa, Asia, Australia, Europe, Latin and North America—there are some 39,000 Mennonite congregations. These people speak dozens of different languages—and their congregations carry diverse names—yet they count themselves as members of one family of faith.

The core of the Anabaptist-Mennonite faith is the belief in Jesus Christ as a model for daily life and in the church as a community which supports its members in living the teachings of Jesus's life and in ministry in the world. Each member's mission is to do his or her part to carry out the mission of Christ in the world. Thus the Mennonite understanding of the nature of "church" is bound up with its understanding of "mission."

The concept of "witness," or example, is also central to the Mennonite faith. Because the tradition holds that the gospel addresses all aspects of life, evangelism and service go hand in hand in believers' day-to-day activities. The emergency relief and development activities conducted worldwide and coordinated by the Mennonite Central Committee embody the values placed both on mission and on witness.

As this family of faith continues to grow, its underlying affirmations remain the same as in the Anabaptist witness of the sixteenth century: separation of church and state, baptism on confession of faith in Jesus Christ, witness against violence, and responsibility to speak against injustice and sin wherever it is found in state and in society.

Adapted by Brenda Wagner from One Family of Faith by Wilbert R. Shenk (Elkhart, Ind.: Council of International Ministries)

History of the Relief Sales

"Right now you have plenty and can help them; then at some other time they can share with you when you need it. In this way each will have as much as he needs."

I Corinthians 8:14

Mennonite Central Committee (MCC) is the cooperative relief, service, and development agency of the North American Mennonite and Brethren in Christ churches. Built on the conviction that meeting human need and service to others are integral parts of the Christian life, this "ministry of reconciliation" seeks to remove the barriers that separate people from each other and from God, and to see that all people share the earth's resources. In this endeavor MCC today coordinates the activities of more than 900 volunteers and staff worldwide.

Although Mennonite congregations in the United States undertook mission work domestically as early as the 1880s and abroad just before the turn of the century, MCC itself was born in 1920 in response to hunger and human need in Russia and Ukraine. Early MCC relief efforts saved many lives there.
In the early 1940s MCC activities expanded in response to the

Thousands of hand-made quilts, donated by church women, are sold at the different relief sales.

agony of war and concern for peace. During World War II, MCC found alternate service opportunities for conscientious objectors, and at the close of the war established relief and refugee programs in Europe. MCC programs expanded in Asia, Africa, and Latin America in the 1950s and 1960s.

Today MCC's volunteers and staff serve two- to three-year assignments in more than 50 countries, including North America. Typically, MCC personnel work closely with local churches and community groups in troubled areas to seek to meet the felt needs of the local people. Assignments include agricultural development, water conservation, health education, participation in village health teams, formal and informal education, economic and technical projects, church-related programs, social services, and peacemaking.

In its work MCC supplies food, necessities, and human and financial resources to war-torn, famine-stricken, and forgotten areas around the globe "in the name of Christ." Much of the food and clothing distributed by MCC is donated by church members. Local committees plan relief sales that support and supplement monies collected through church offerings and generated by thrift shops. The concept of the relief sale—a prime source of funds to support

*The quilt sales draw visitors from miles around and out-of-state—
eager for quality quilts at very reasonable prices.*

Making Relief Sales Strawberry Pies (see recipe on page 115). Over one million such strawberry pies have been sold over the years.

MCC efforts—first appeared in the early 1920s. In the spring of 1922, on the John K. Warkentin farm south of Reedley, California, a sale was held to raise funds for Siberian Mennonites suffering from famine. Between $200 and $300 was raised, planting the seed for subsequent Mennonite relief sale efforts.

The first "official" Mennonite relief sale was held in Gap, Pennsylvania, in 1957. The idea spread, with central Ontario holding its first sale in 1967. From these humble beginnings, the relief sale phenomenon has developed into a vast grassroots effort across Canada and the United States to raise financial resources to support the work of the MCC. In 1992 Pennsylvania held its 36th Annual Relief Sale and Ontario, its 26th Annual Sale.

Proceeds from all North American sales are donated directly to the Mennonite Central Committee. In 1992, 36 relief sales in the United States and Canada contributed $4.1 million to MCC service activities.

Held through-out the year, Mennonite relief sales provide a vehicle

A view from the auction platform

through which members of Mennonite and Brethren in Christ congregations can give of their time, talent, and money to help the less fortunate. Throughout the year before each sale, quilts and other crafts, including needlework, pottery, woodwork, and paintings, are made in group gatherings in churches and homes and individually. Antiques and other quality used items are donated. In the days just before the sale, thousands of pies, cookies, cakes, breads, and rolls are baked for sale along with home-preserved jams, jellies, pickles, and relishes. Food and small items are sold from booths by volunteers during the sale, while quilts, furniture and sometimes livestock are sold at auction. Many Mennonites see these relief sales as "festivals" of service.

This cookbook contains treasured recipes from Mennonite families. Among them are instructions for making many of the foodstuffs one will find at Mennonite relief sales. Mennonite food traditions vary—and reflect both the cultures from which various Mennonite groups came (Swiss, German, Dutch, Russian, Polish) and the influence of their current geography.
Although food itself is in no way part of the Mennonite religious

Feeding the hungry multitudes at the
Kansas City relief sale.

faith, respect for the land and its bounty is strong. And the function of the church as community provides many opportunities for the sharing of food in social contexts.

> *Adapted by Brenda Wagner from MCC*
> *Relief Sales: From the Past to the*
> *Present compiled by Menno L. Kliewer*
> *and edited by Stephen Penner*

Yeast Breads

White Bread

Scald 2 cups milk
Add 4 tablespoons sugar
    2 tablespoons salt
    4 tablespoons shortening
Stir till all is dissolved.
Cool to lukewarm.

In a separate bowl put
1 cup lukewarm water
1 teaspoon sugar, stir to dissolve, sprinkle
1 package yeast over and let stand 10
minutes. Then beat with a fork and add
to first mixture.
Add 2 beaten eggs and 2 cups
cold potato water.
Stir in 4 cups all-purpose flour and beat well.
Then work in about 10 more cups flour and
knead 200 times. Let rise in warm place until
double, work down and let rise again. Shape
into loaves and let rise again. Bake at 275°
for about one hour. Brush hot loaves with
melted butter.

Whole Wheat Bread

Scald 1½ cups milk. Pour into a large bowl and add ½ cup brown sugar or
molasses, 2 tablespoons salt, ½ cup shortening. Stir till shortening melts. Add
2¼ cups water. Cool to lukewarm.

Meanwhile dissolve 2 teaspoons sugar in 1 cup lukewarm water (100°). Over this
sprinkle 2 envelopes (or 2 tablespoons) active dry yeast. Let stand 10 minutes.
Stir briskly with a fork. Add softened yeast to lukewarm milk mixture. Stir.

Beat in 6 cups whole wheat flour. Beat vigorously by hand or with electric mixer,
then gradually beat in with spoon 6–6½ cups all-purpose flour. Work in last of
flour with a rotating motion of hand.

Turn dough on floured surface and knead 9–10 minutes. Shape into smooth ball
and place in greased bowl, rotating dough to grease surface. Cover with a damp
cloth and let rise till doubled (about 1¼ hours). Keep in a warm place. Punch
down and shape into 4 loaves. Place in greased 8½x4½ inch loaf pans, let rise
again until doubled (about 1 hour). Bake in 375° oven for about 35 minutes.

*God gives us the ingredients for our daily
bread, but He expects <u>us</u> to do the baking!*

Rolled Oat Bread

2 cups milk
1 cup rolled oats (oatmeal)
2 tablespoons white sugar
2 teaspoons salt
3 tablespoons lard
2 tablespoons refined molasses
½ cup lukewarm water
1 teaspoon white sugar
1 envelope dry yeast
3¾-4 cups all-purpose flour

Scald milk, add oatmeal, 2 tablespoons sugar, salt, lard, molasses and cool to lukewarm. Dissolve 1 teaspoon white sugar in ½ cup warm water and sprinkle yeast over, let stand 10 minutes. Add yeast to milk and oatmeal mixture and 1 cup flour and beat well until smooth and elastic.

Work in remaining flour until a smooth soft dough. Let rise to double in bulk. Punch down and form into 2 equal portions and let rest 10 minutes, then shape into loaves, let rise again to double in bulk. Bake in 350° oven for 1 hour. Makes 2 good sized loaves.

Basic Sweet Dough

Scald 1½ cups milk.
Add ¼ cup white sugar, 2¼ teaspoons salt, ¾ cup shortening. Stir to dissolve, cool to lukewarm.
Into a large bowl measure ¾ cup lukewarm water, 1 tablespoon white sugar, stir till dissolved. Sprinkle with 3 envelopes yeast (3 tablespoons). Let stand 10 minutes, beat with fork.
Stir yeast mixture into milk mixture. Add 3 well beaten eggs.
Stir in 4 cups all-purpose flour and beat till smooth and elastic, then work in about 3 more cups flour. Turn on slightly floured board and knead lightly until smooth (about 5 minutes). Place in a greased bowl and lightly grease top of dough. Let rise in warm place free from draft until double in bulk (about 1½ hours).

Use this Basic Sweet Dough recipe for Coffee Cake, Cinnamon Rolls, Chelsea Buns, etc. Instructions on pages 5–6.

Women are made to be loved—
not understood.

Swedish Tea Ring

Roll out ¼ of Basic Sweet Dough (page 4) about 14x9 inches. Spread with melted butter. Sprinkle ⅓ cup brown sugar and ⅓ cup blanched almonds (or raisins) and 1 to 2 tablespoons mixed cut citrus peel. Roll up lengthwise jelly roll fashion. Shape into a circle, seam side down on greased baking sheet. With scissors cut ring ⅔ of the way through from the outside edge about 1 inch apart, turn slices partly to one side overlapping each other. Cover and let rise until doubled. Bake at 375° about 25 minutes. When cool, drizzle with icing made with 1 cup powdered sugar, 2 tablespoons milk and ½ teaspoon vanilla. Garnish with chopped nuts or maraschino cherries.

Cinnamon Rolls

Use ¼ of Basic Sweet Dough (page 4) and roll into 9x12 inch rectangle and brush with melted butter. Sprinkle with ½ cup of brown sugar and 2 teaspoons cinnamon. Roll up tightly, beginning at wide side. Seal edge well. Cut into 12 slices and place in well greased rectangle pan. Let rise till double. Bake at 350° about 30 minutes.

Jam Ring

Roll out portion of Basic Sweet Dough (page 4) 16x8 inches. Spread with ⅓ cup nuts. Roll up loosely. Twist dough from end to end and form into a ring on greased pan. Let rise till double and bake at 325° 25 to 30 minutes. Spread hot ring with white icing and decorate top.

Chelsea Buns

Follow instructions for Cinnamon Rolls (above), sprinkling ½ cup raisins before rolling up dough. Cut into 9 slices. Into an 8 inch square pan put the following: ⅓ cup melted butter, sprinkle ½ cup brown sugar over, also pecans or walnuts, then arrange the 9 slices in pan. Let rise till double and bake at 350° about 30 minutes. Turn upside down on a wire rack for 5 minutes to allow syrup to run over buns.

Cream Buns

Shape ¼ of Basic Sweet Dough (page 4) into 12 equal parts and place in a rectangular greased pan. Let rise till double, then bake at 375° about 25 minutes. While hot, brush with melted butter. Just before serving slit buns and fill with the following: ¼ cup shortening, ½ cup milk and 3 cups powdered sugar and 1 teaspoon vanilla. Beat till fluffy.

Coffee Cake

Shape Basic Sweet Dough (page 4) into pans, brush top with cream, then sprinkle with brown sugar. Let rise till double, then bake at 375° 30 minutes.

Quick Water Bread

This can be made in less time than it takes to go to the store.

1 package dry yeast
1 cup water
1 tablespoon white sugar
4 cups all-purpose flour
2 teaspoons salt

Dissolve sugar in the water which should be lukewarm, sprinkle yeast on top and let stand 10 minutes. Stir. Sift flour and salt into separate bowl. Add yeast mixture. Add just enough water to make a soft dough—about ⅓ cup. Stir well. Let rise until double in bulk. Divide dough in half and place in two buttered casseroles. Let rise again. Bake in 400° oven for about 40 minutes.

Oatmeal Rolls

Dissolve 2 packages dry yeast into ¾ cup warm water. In a mixing bowl put ½ cup shortening, ½ cup brown sugar, 3 teaspoons salt, and 2 cups quick oatmeal. Scald 2 cups milk and pour over this mixture. Cool to lukewarm. Add 2 beaten eggs and yeast mixture, then beat in 1 cup all-purpose flour. Let stand about 15 minutes till bubbly and light, then work in about 5 more cups flour, knead till a soft dough. Place in greased bowl and let rise till double. Punch down and let rise again. Work into rolls. Let rise again and bake at 400° for 10 minutes.

Refrigerator Rolls

Part 1
¾ cup lard, 1 cup boiling water. Pour over lard to melt it. Add 1 cup cold water, 1 tablespoon salt.

Part 2
½ cup white sugar, 2 eggs beaten, 2 packages yeast dissolved in 1 cup warm water, let stand 10 minutes. Mix parts 1 and 2 and add 7 cups all-purpose flour, more if needed. Set in refrigerator till needed. After putting in pans, let rise 3 hours. Then bake. Dough keeps a week in refrigerator.

Plucketts

1 package yeast, ½ cup lukewarm water, 1 teaspoon sugar. Dissolve sugar in water, sprinkle yeast on top, let stand 10 minutes.
Mix together well: ⅓ cup scalded milk, 2 tablespoons white sugar, 1 tablespoon shortening, 1 teaspoon salt. Add a bit of flour to milk mixture, then 1 beaten egg and a bit more flour, then beat in yeast mixture, then rest of flour (about 2¼ cups altogether), knead till elastic (8 to 10 minutes). Let rise till double, about 2 hours. Combine ½ cup white sugar, 1¼ teaspoon cinnamon, ½ cup finely chopped nuts together. Melt ⅓ cup butter. Punch down dough and cut into 24 pieces. Roll each piece in hand, then in butter, then in sugar mixture. Put in well greased 9 inch square or a tube cake pan about 1½ or 2 layers. (Do not place too close together, second layer in alternate spaces). Let rise till double (1½ to 2 hours). Bake at 350° till done. Serve warm. Can be reheated before serving.

Hungarian Walnut Strudel

½ cup lukewarm milk
1 package yeast
1 tablespoon sugar
1½ cups all-purpose flour
½ cup butter
3 egg yolks
juice ½ lemon
2 tablespoons sour cream

Sift flour and cut in butter. (Sprinkle yeast in lukewarm milk plus sugar and let stand 10 minutes.) Make a well in flour mixture and add egg yolks, lemon juice and 2 tablespoons sour cream, and yeast mixture. Mix by hand adding more flour to make a dough that doesn't stick to the fingers. Knead on lightly floured board rolling and folding until shiny. Roll out half of dough to ½ inch thickness and spread with walnut filling. Roll up and place edge down on well greased pan. Let rise for 1 hour. Brush with egg yolk. Bake at 375° for ½ hour. Turn oven off and let stand 15 minutes longer.

Walnut Filling: ½ pound walnuts, 3 egg whites, ¾ cup sugar, 2 tablespoons fine dry bread crumbs, pinch salt
Beat egg whites with salt until stiff and add sugar gradually, beating. Fold in ground walnuts, and bread crumbs.

Triumph is just a little 'try' and a lot of 'umph'.

Quick Breads
(Tea Breads, Muffins, Pancakes, Donuts)

Apricot Brazil Bread

Soak ½ cup coarsely chopped dried apricots (packed) in ¼ cup water for
30 minutes.
In large mixing bowl beat until foamy 1 egg, 1 cup granulated sugar.
Stir in ¼ cup melted butter or margarine, 1 cup orange juice.
Sift together 2 cups sifted all-purpose flour, ½ teaspoon salt, 3 teaspoons baking
powder, ¼ teaspoon baking soda.
Stir in 1 cup chopped brazil nuts or walnuts.

Add dry ingredients to first mixture, along with soaked apricots and water. Beat
well. Turn into well greased loaf pan, smoothing top.
Bake at 350° for 60 minutes.
Cool in pan 10 minutes. Turn out and cool on rack.

Applesauce Nut Bread

Sift together into mixing bowl:
1½ cups flour
1 teaspoon baking powder
1 teaspoon soda
1 teaspoon salt
1 teaspoon cinnamon
½ teaspoon nutmeg
Stir in:
1 cup oatmeal
1 cup chopped walnuts
½ cup raisins
Cream:
⅓ cup shortening
½ cup brown sugar

Add 2 eggs and beat until light and fluffy.
Blend in 1 cup unsweetened applesauce
and ½ cup milk.
Add creamed mixture to dry ingredients
and beat ½ minute. (Do not overbeat, can
be lumpy.)
Bake at 350° for 50–60 minutes.

Chop nuts the easy way—put between layers
of wax paper and roll with a rolling pin.

Banana Nut Bread

⅔ cup shortening
2½ cups sifted cake flour
1⅔ cups sugar
1¼ teaspoons baking powder
1 teaspoon soda
1 teaspoon salt
1¼ cups mashed very ripe
   bananas (about 3)
⅔ cup buttermilk
2 eggs
⅔ cup chopped walnuts

Stir shortening just to soften. Sift dry ingredients into same bowl. Add bananas and half of buttermilk. Mix until all flour is dampened, then beat vigorously for 2 minutes. Add remaining buttermilk and eggs and beat 2 minutes longer. Fold in slightly floured nuts. Bake in 2 wax paper lined lightly greased loaf pans.
Bake at 350° for 35 minutes. Can also be baked in 8 inch square cake pan or as cupcakes.

Carrot Bread

½ cup salad oil
1 cup sugar
2 eggs, beaten
1 cup shredded carrots
1½ cups sifted all-purpose
   flour
1 teaspoon soda
1 teaspoon baking powder
¼ teaspoon salt
1 teaspoon cinnamon
½ cup milk
½ cup chopped walnuts
   (optional)

Mix sugar and salad oil. Add beaten eggs. Stir in shredded carrots. Sift flour, baking powder, soda, salt and cinnamon. Add small amounts to sugar mixture alternately with milk. Stir in walnuts if desired. Bake in a 9x5x3 inch well greased loaf pan for 55 minutes in a 350° oven.

Many are called, but few get up for breakfast.

Cherry Tea Bread

¼ cup margarine or butter
¾ cup white sugar
⅛ teaspoon almond flavoring
½ cup well drained red
   maraschino cherries, halved
1 egg, well beaten
2 cups sifted all-purpose flour
2½ teaspoons baking powder
½ teaspoon salt
¾ cup milk

Cream margarine and sugar and flavoring, when smooth add egg and cherries, mix well, then add sifted dry ingredients alternately with milk. Do not overbeat. Pour batter in well greased loaf pan. Bake at 325° for 1 hour. While still hot brush top of loaf with margarine or butter to prevent cracking. Loaf slices better after 24 hours.

Dutch Honey Bread

1 cup honey
1 cup brown sugar
1⅓ cups milk, scalded

Pour the hot milk over honey and sugar and stir until dissolved in a large mixing bowl.

Sift together:
4 cups pastry flour
1 teaspoon cinnamon
2 teaspoons baking soda
½ teaspoon cloves

Stir dry ingredients into liquid mixture, do not overbeat. Pour into loaf pan lined with wax paper. Bake in 350° oven for 1 hour.
Cool upside down on rack before removing wax paper.

Good talkers have little trouble getting jobs, but only good doers keep them!

Lemon Tea Bread

⅓ cup shortening
1 cup white sugar
2 eggs, well beaten
½ cup milk
1 teaspoon baking powder
⅛ teaspoon salt
2 cups flour
½ cup walnuts
2 teaspoons lemon juice
1 teaspoon lemon rind

Cream shortening and sugar well and add beaten eggs. Sift only 1 cup of flour and baking powder and salt and add to creamed mixture, then blend in milk, lemon rind and juice and nuts, now blend in the remaining 1 cup of sifted flour. Pour into greased loaf pan and bake at 300° for 90 minutes. While hot, spread loaf with the following mixture:

2 teaspoons sugar
2 teaspoons lemon rind
1 teaspoon lemon juice

Mincemeat Tea Bread

2 cups all-purpose flour
½ cup sugar
1½ teaspoons baking powder
½ teaspoon soda
½ teaspoon salt
1 egg, lightly beaten
¼ cup oil or melted shortening
1 tablespoon grated
   orange rind
2 tablespoons orange juice
2 cups (16 ounces)
   mincemeat

Sift dry ingredients together. Combine liquids and mincemeat and add to dry ingredients. Stir until all ingredients are moistened (17 to 22 strokes). Bake in a greased 9x5x3 inch loaf pan at 350° for 60 to 65 minutes.

Some men are so busy earning bread for
their children that they forget
that a child does not live by bread alone.

Pumpkin Bread

1¾ cups flour
1½ cups sugar
1 teaspoon soda
¾ teaspoon salt
½ teaspoon cloves
½ teaspoon cinnamon
½ teaspoon nutmeg
Sift dry ingredients into mixing bowl, then add:
½ cup salad oil
⅓ cup water
1 cup pumpkin
2 eggs, beaten
½ cup chopped nuts
½ cup raisins
Put in greased loaf pan or soup or vegetable tins half full. Bake at 350°
35–40 minutes.

Moist Date Bran Loaf

Pour 2 cups boiling water over 1 pound cut up dates and 1 teaspoon soda.
Let stand until almost cool.
Add 3 tablespoons soft butter and 1 teaspoon vanilla.
Now add 1½ cups brown sugar and ½ cup (or more) chopped nuts and 1 cup
natural health bran. Sift and add 2 cups flour, 2 teaspoons baking powder and
1 teaspoon salt. Mix together.
Bake 1 hour at 350°. Makes 2 loaves.
This is a moist dark bread and keeps much better than a secret.
Freezes well too.

Date Nut Muffins

2 cups whole wheat flour
⅔ cup all-purpose flour
2 teaspoons soda
1 teaspoon salt
1⅓ cups white sugar
2 eggs
1 cup salad oil
1½ cups milk
1 teaspoon maple flavoring *or*
    ⅓ teaspoon cinnamon
3 ounces applesauce
⅓ cup chopped dates
1 cup chopped walnuts

Sift first five ingredients together into mixing bowl. Mix all wet ingredients in another bowl, now combine both mixtures and add nuts and dates. Stir until blended and smooth. Put in greased muffin tins and bake at 400° for 20 minutes. Makes 2 dozen muffins.

Bran Muffins *(quick mix method)*

Into a bowl measure 1 cup bran, 1 cup brown sugar. Sift on top 1 cup all-purpose flour, 1 teaspoon baking powder, ½ teaspoon soda.
Make a cavity in center of it all. Pour into it ½ cup oil, 1 egg and 1 cup buttermilk or sour milk. Stir until mixed, no more.

Raisins or dates may be added. If using raisins, measure and cover with boiling water when starting to mix the batter to plump them. Drain well before adding.

Bake at 375° about 15 minutes.
Yield: 1½ dozen
They freeze well if you can get them to the freezer!

What wisdom can you find that is greater than kindness?

Banana Muffins

1 egg
½ cup white sugar
1 cup mashed bananas
1½ cups flour
¾ teaspoon soda
½ teaspoon baking powder
½ teaspoon salt
¼ cup melted butter
½ cup broken walnuts

Cream egg and sugar, add mashed bananas. Sift dry ingredients together and blend with first mixture. Add melted butter and walnuts and mix lightly. Bake in greased muffin tins. Bake at 350° for 20 minutes. (This recipe can also be baked in a cake pan.)

Oatmeal Muffins

1 cup flour
¼ cup white sugar
3 teaspoons baking powder
½ teaspoon salt
3 tablespoons shortening
1 cup quick cooking oatmeal
½ cup chopped dates or raisins
1 egg (well beaten)
1 cup milk

Sift flour, sugar, baking powder and salt. Into this mixture cut in the shortening, then add oatmeal and dates and blend well. Add milk and beaten egg and mix lightly. Fill greased muffin tins ⅔ full and bake at 425° till done. Makes 1 dozen muffins.

Tea Biscuits

2 eggs, 1 cup sweet cream, ½ teaspoon salt, 2 teaspoons baking powder, 1¾ cups all-purpose flour. Put unbeaten eggs in mixing bowl, add cream, salt, then flour which has been sifted with baking powder, stir well and drop on greased cookie sheet or bake in square 8x8 inch pan.
For shortcake bake in pie plate. Bake at 375° 20 minutes.

There is as much greatness in acknowledging
a good turn as in doing it.

Easy Scones

2 cups flour
4 teaspoons baking powder
2 teaspoons sugar
⅓ cup milk or cream
½ teaspoon salt
4 tablespoons butter or
  margarine
2 eggs

Sift dry ingredients. Work in butter with pastry mixer or fork; add milk and well beaten eggs (reserve a small amount of unbeaten egg white). Toss on floured board, pat and roll ¾ inch thick.
Cut in squares, diamonds or triangles, brush with reserved egg white diluted with 1 teaspoon water. Sprinkle with sugar and bake for 15 minutes in 450° oven. Makes 12 scones.

Johnny Cake I

Mix together: 1 egg, 1 cup sugar, 1 cup cream (sweet or sour), dissolve 1 teaspoon soda in cream. Add: 1½ cup cornmeal, 1 cup flour, 1 teaspoon salt. Bake in 9x9 inch pan at 350° about 40 minutes. Can also use muffin tins.

Johnny Cake II

Cream together: ¼ cup shortening, ½ cup sugar, 1 egg. Sift 1 cup all-purpose flour and 2½ teaspoons baking powder, and ½ teaspoon salt. Add 1 cup cornmeal. Mix 1 cup milk alternately with dry ingredients. Bake at 375° in 9x9 inch pan or muffin tins about 40 minutes.

Doughnuts

Into a mixing bowl sift 3½ cups pastry flour, 4 teaspoons baking powder, and 1 cup fine sugar. Make a well in the center and add 3 tablespoons soft butter or margarine, 2 egg yolks, ¾ cup + 2 tablespoons milk, vanilla and nutmeg to taste. Beat. Finally add 2 well beaten egg whites. Cut or shape and fry in fat 350° until nice and brown on both sides.

German Buns

4 cups sifted all-purpose flour
1 teaspoon salt
1 cup white sugar
1 teaspoon soda
2 teaspoons cream of tartar
Sift dry ingredients together into mixing bowl and then add:
1 egg, well beaten
½ cup lard
½ cup butter
Mix to a soft dough with:
¼ cup milk and ¼ cup water
Roll to ½ inch thickness and spread with the following mixture:
1 egg, beaten
1 cup brown sugar
½ cup flour
Roll up like a jelly roll and cut in slices. Place in greased pan, not too close as they spread. Bake at 375° for 8–10 minutes.

Relief Sale Doughnuts

Dissolve 1 package yeast in
    1 cup warm water.

1 cup mashed potatoes
1 cup lard
1 cup scalded milk
½ cup sugar
2 eggs
flour

Mix in order given and add enough flour so dough will not stick to fingers. Let rise until double in bulk. Roll out and cut; put on trays which have some flour on. Let rise again, then fry, drain, then dip in syrup: 1 pound powdered sugar, ½ cup water. Dip while still hot.

No man (or woman) will ever be a great leader who does not take genuine joy in the success of those under him.

Relief Sale Teaballs

Mix on the beater:
2 eggs, 1 cup brown sugar, 1 cup light whipping cream, 1 cup buttermilk,
1 teaspoon soda, ¼ teaspoon nutmeg, ½ teaspoon orange flavor. Add and stir
only enough to blend: 3 cups all-purpose flour, 1 teaspoon baking powder, 1
teaspoon salt.
Drop by spoonfuls into fat 350° until light brown. Best results are when cream
and buttermilk are unpasteurized.

Teaballs

3 eggs
1 cup sugar
1 cup milk
2 tablespoons melted fat
½ teaspoon vanilla
½ teaspoon nutmeg
½ teaspoon salt
2 teaspoons baking powder
2 cups flour

Beat eggs. Add sugar, vanilla and milk. Add
sifted dry ingredients. Beat well and then add
warm fat. Drop by spoonfuls into hot fat
350°–365°.

Apple Fritters (Relief Sale)

Sift together:
2 cups all-purpose flour
2 tablespoons sugar
1 teaspoon salt
3 teaspoons baking powder

Beat 2 eggs slightly in a 2-cup measuring cup.
Add milk to 2-cup level. Beat all together with
beater. Blender works too. Dip apple rings in
batter. Fry in deep fat at 375°. Electric fry pan
works well.

A woman can throw more out the back door
than her husband can bring in the front.

Buttermilk Pancakes

2 cups buttermilk
2 cups flour
3 tablespoons butter
1 teaspoon baking powder
½ teaspoon salt
1 teaspoon soda
2 teaspoons sugar
2 eggs

Sift dry ingredients, add buttermilk, beat till smooth. Add egg yolks and melted butter, fold in beaten egg whites. Bake on hot slightly greased griddle until golden brown.

Griddle Cakes

1 egg
1 cup milk
½ teaspoon salt
1 cup bread flour
2 teaspoons baking powder
1½ tablespoons melted
    shortening

Beat egg and add milk. Sift flour with baking powder and salt and beat into mixture, add shortening last. Drop by tablespoon on hot griddle and brown on both sides. Serve with maple syrup.

Whole Wheat Pancakes

2 eggs
1 cup brown sugar
1 tablespoon butter
½ teaspoon salt
2 teaspoons baking powder
1 cup milk
2 cups whole wheat flour

Beat eggs, add sugar and milk. Sift dry ingredients and add to liquid. Add melted shortening and blend together. Bake on hot lightly greased griddle or pan.
Makes 8–10 pancakes.

Apple Pancakes

3 tablespoons flour
1 egg
pinch of salt
sweet milk, enough to make
    batter a little thicker than
    cream (¼–⅓ cup)

2 apples chopped—not too fine, and need not be peeled. Fry in a covered pan in order to cook the apples. This batter is very thin and will spread over entire pan. Cut in four and turn as best you can.
Serves 2.

Sour Cream Coffee Cake

Topping—mix and set aside
1 cup chopped pecans
    (or walnuts)
½ cup butter (melted)
¼ cup white sugar
⅓ cup brown sugar
1 teaspoon cinnamon

Batter
½ cup shortening
1 cup sugar.
2 eggs
1 teaspoon vanilla
Mix 2 cups flour
1 teaspoon baking powder
1 teaspoon soda
½ teaspoon salt
1 cup sour cream

Cream shortening and sugar, beat in eggs and vanilla. Mix dry ingredients and alternately add the batter (half at a time) with 1 cup sour cream (half at a time).
Put half the *topping* in a greased tube pan, then add half the batter. Repeat. Bake at 350° for 45 minutes or until done. Let cool for 5 minutes before turning out on a rack. Keeps well.

The time to make friends is
before you need them.

Cakes and
Frostings

Lazy Daisy Oatmeal Cake

1¼ cups boiling water
1 cup oatmeal
½ cup shortening
1 cup white sugar
1 cup brown sugar (packed)
1 teaspoon vanilla
2 eggs
1½ cups sifted flour
1 teaspoon soda
½ teaspoon salt
¾ teaspoon cinnamon
¼ teaspoon nutmeg

Pour water over oatmeal, cover and let stand 20 minutes. Beat shortening until creamy; gradually add sugars and beat until fluffy. Blend in vanilla and eggs. Add oat mixture, mix well. Sift together dry ingredients and add to creamed mixture; mix well. Pour into well greased and floured 9 inch pan. Bake at 350° for about 50 minutes.

Topping
¼ cup melted butter
½ cup brown sugar
3 tablespoons cream
⅓ cup chopped nutmeats
¾ cup coconut

Combine all ingredients and spread over warm cake. Broil until frosting becomes bubbly and lightly browned.

Queen Elizabeth Cake

1 cup boiling water
1 cup chopped dates
1 teaspoon baking soda
¼ cup shortening
1 cup white sugar
1 egg
1 teaspoon vanilla
½ cup walnuts
1½ cups flour
1½ teaspoons baking powder
¼ teaspoon salt

Add soda to dates, pour boiling water over, let cool. Cream shortening, add sugar, cream well. Beat in egg, vanilla, and salt. Add flour, baking powder and nuts alternately with date mixture. Bake at 350° for 1 hour in 8x12 inch pan.

Topping
¼ cup melted butter
½ cup brown sugar
3 tablespoons cream
⅓ cup chopped nutmeats
¾ cup coconut

Combine all ingredients and spread over warm cake. Broil until frosting becomes bubbly and lightly browned.

Banana Cake *(one bowl method)*

Measure into large
   mixing bowl:
⅔ cup soft shortening
all of sifted dry ingredients:
2½ cups cake flour
1⅔ cups sugar
1¼ teaspoons baking powder
1 teaspoon soda
1 teaspoon salt
1¼ cups mashed bananas
⅓ cup buttermilk
2 eggs

Using beater blend all and then beat 2 minutes on medium speed. Add ⅓ cup buttermilk and 2 eggs. Beat 2 minutes longer. Bake in two 9 inch layer pans or a 9x13 inch pan at 350°.

Quick and easy and good!

Maple-Nut Chiffon Cake

2 cups sifted cake flour
1½ cups white sugar
3 teaspoons baking powder
1 teaspoon salt
½ cup salad oil
6 egg yolks
¾ cup cold water
2 teaspoons maple flavoring
6 egg whites
1 cup ground walnuts
½ teaspoon cream of tartar

Sift first four ingredients together. Add in order given the next four ingredients. Beat until satin smooth. In large bowl combine egg whites and cream of tartar. Beat until *very* stiff peaks form. Pour egg yolk batter in thin stream over egg whites, gently fold in till blended. Fold in nuts. Bake in 10 inch ungreased tube pan 60–65 minutes at 350°.

Icing
1 egg
¼ cup butter
¼ cup milk
1 teaspoon maple flavoring
1 pound powdered sugar

Beat first four ingredients until fluffy. Add powdered sugar. Spread on cake.

Two-Egg Chiffon Cake

2 eggs, separated
1½ cups sugar
2½ cups sifted cake flour
3 teaspoons baking powder
1 teaspoon salt
⅓ cup salad oil
1 cup milk
1½ teaspoons vanilla

Beat egg whites until frothy, gradually beat in ½ cup sugar. Beat until stiff. Sift remaining sugar, flour, baking powder, salt into another bowl. Pour in oil, half of milk. Beat 1 minute at medium speed. Add remaining milk, egg yolks, flavoring. Beat 1 minute more. Fold meringue into batter by cutting gently through batter. Pour into 2 round layer pans or one oblong pan that is greased and dusted with flour. Heat oven to 350°. Bake layers 25 to 35 minutes, oblong 35 to 40 minutes. This is good also for cupcakes.

Easy Icing

Into a large bowl put
    the following:
1 egg white
few grains of salt
½ teaspoon cream of tartar
1 cup white sugar
1 teaspoon vanilla
½ cup boiling water

Beat 7–9 minutes, and it's done.
No boiling.
Enough for large cake.
Use same day.

Sour Cream Spice Cake

1 cup brown sugar
1 egg
1 cup sour cream
½ cup raisins
1½ cups sifted flour
½ teaspoon cream of tartar
½ teaspoon salt
1 teaspoon cinnamon
½ teaspoon cloves
1 teaspoon baking soda

Beat sugar and egg. Stir in sour cream, then raisins, add dry ingredients. Spread evenly in greased 9x9 inch pan. Bake about 25 minutes at 350°.

Cakes and Frostings

Black Chocolate Cake

2 cups sifted cake flour
1 cup white sugar
2 teaspoons soda
½ teaspoon salt
¼ cup cocoa
1 cup cold water
1 cup salad dressing
1 teaspoon vanilla

Mix dry ingredients. Blend in wet ingredients; do not beat. Bake at 350° for at least 45 minutes, or until the center springs back when touched. Cool, then spread with Mocha Icing (recipe below).

Mocha Icing

2 tablespoons butter
2 tablespoons cocoa
½ cup powdered sugar
3 tablespoons strong hot coffee
¼ teaspoon vanilla
pinch of salt

Mix and spread on Black Chocolate Cake (recipe above).

Fruit Cocktail Cake

Beat together:
2 large eggs
1½ cups white sugar
Sift together:
2 cups unsifted
    all-purpose flour
2 teaspoons soda

Add dry ingredients to first mixture alternately with 1 can (14 ounces) fruit cocktail (include syrup). Bake at 350° in 9x13 inch pan.

Topping
Mix together in small
    saucepan:
¼ pound butter
1 cup white sugar
½ cup evaporated milk
1 cup coconut
1 teaspoon vanilla
¾ cup chopped nuts

Boil together 2 minutes and spread on warm cake. A strange-sounding recipe, but a favorite of those with a sweet tooth.

Marble Chiffon Cake

Stir until smooth and set aside until later:
½ cup cocoa
¼ cup white sugar
¼ cup boiling water
¼ teaspoon red food coloring

Step one
Measure and sift into small bowl:
2¼ cups cake flour
1½ cups sugar
1 teaspoon salt
3 teaspoons baking powder
Make a well and add in order:
½ cup corn oil
5 unbeaten egg yolks
¾ cup cold water
2 teaspoons vanilla
Beat until smooth.

Step two
Measure into large bowl:
½ teaspoon cream of tartar
1 cup egg whites
Beat until very stiff.

Step three
Pour egg yolk mixture gradually over egg whites. Gently fold just until blended.
Do not stir. Place half of batter into another bowl, pour cocoa mixture over it,
blend. Immediately pour alternate layers of dark and white batter into
ungreased tube pan. Bake at 325° for 55 minutes.

Clean coffee percolator by perking
baking soda in water. Rinse thoroughly.

Grandma's Cocoa Cake

1 egg
1 cup sugar
½ cup lard
1 teaspoon salt
5 teaspoons cocoa (heaping)
1 cup sour milk
1 teaspoon soda
2 cups (scant) flour
1 teaspoon vanilla

Mix in order given. Bake in a slow oven.

Graham Wafer Cake

1 cup white sugar
½ cup shortening or butter
1 egg
2 cups graham wafer crumbs
   (rolled fine)
2 tablespoons flour
1½ teaspoons baking powder
1 cup coconut
1 cup milk
vanilla
pinch of salt

Beat sugar, shortening and egg. Add milk and dry ingredients. Bake 45 minutes at 350°.

Note: Vanilla wafers can be used—good flavor too.

Topping for Cake
2 cups brown sugar
4 tablespoons butter or
   margarine
2 tablespoons flour
6 tablespoons cream or milk
vanilla

Cook topping ingredients (except vanilla) until they boil, then boil one minute and remove from heat. Add vanilla and beat until shine begins to disappear. Spread quickly.

Wacky Cake

3 cups flour
2 cups sugar
½ cup cocoa
2 teaspoons soda
1 teaspoon salt
2 tablespoons vinegar
2 teaspoons vanilla
⅔ cup salad oil
2 cups water

Sift into 9x12 ungreased pan the first five ingredients. Mix and make three holes. Pour vinegar, vanilla, salad oil into holes. Over top pour water and mix until all ingredients are blended. Bake at 350° for 30–35 minutes.

Sauerkraut Cake

2¼ cups all-purpose flour
½ cup cocoa
1 teaspoon baking powder
1 teaspoon soda
¼ teaspoon salt
⅔ cup sauerkraut
    (drained and rinsed)
⅔ cup butter
1½ cups sugar
3 large eggs
1 teaspoon vanilla
1 cup strong coffee
    (cool) or water

Combine first five ingredients. Cream butter and sugar, add one egg at a time. Add vanilla, then liquid and dry ingredients alternately, beginning and ending with flour. Stir in sauerkraut and bake at 350° for 20–25 minutes in 9x13 inch or layer cake pans.

Grandmother Cressman's Applesauce Cake

½ cup + 1 tablespoon
  shortening
1 cup brown sugar
1 egg, beaten
2 cups sifted pastry flour
1 teaspoon soda
3 tablespoons cocoa
½ teaspoon salt
1 teaspoon cinnamon
¼ teaspoon cloves
1 cup applesauce
  (unsweetened preferred)
1 cup chopped raisins,
  slightly floured

Cream shortening and add sugar gradually, beating until light. Add beaten egg and beat again. Add sifted dry ingredients alternately with applesauce and lastly fold in raisins. Bake in loaf or square or cupcakes at 350°. Very moist and good for lunch boxes.

Almond Torte

½ pound unblanched
  almonds, finely ground
1 cup sugar
6 eggs (whole)
5 egg whites, beaten stiff
1 teaspoon baking powder
1 cup fine dry bread crumbs

Beat sugar into whole eggs. Add almonds, crumbs and baking powder. Fold in egg whites. Pour into shallow cake pan. Bake at 325° until done. Cool completely.

Filling
1 cup milk
1 cup triple strength coffee
1 package vanilla pudding
1 package unflavored gelatin
1 cup whipping cream

Add milk and coffee to commercial vanilla pudding, mix and bring to boil.
During boiling, soak one package of plain gelatin in cold water. Add to pudding, stirring occasionally to avoid lumps. Cool completely. Whip 1 cup whipping cream and fold into pudding.

Slice cake and spread with mixture in centers and on top. Garnish with finely grated chocolate.

Icing

1 cup milk
5 tablespoons flour
½–1 cup shortening
1 cup sugar
salt
vanilla

Mix milk and flour and boil until very thick. Cool. Beat shortening, add sugar and beat until fluffy. Add this to cooked mixture slowly, then beat for 15 minutes. Add salt and vanilla. This will keep in refrigerator for weeks and is ready to use any time.

Sauce for Angel Food Cake

½ cup white sugar
2 tablespoons cornstarch
1 egg
1 cup pineapple juice
    or diluted lemon juice

Cook over low heat until mixture thickens. Remove from heat and cool. Mix with one envelope prepared whipped topping mix.

Chocolate Icing

In pan melt ¼ cup butter, ¼ cup cocoa. Put into small mixer bowl. Start beater and add alternately ¼ cup milk, vanilla to taste, and enough powdered sugar to make desired consistency.

Maple Cream Icing

1 cup brown sugar
3 tablespoons milk
1 tablespoon butter
powdered sugar
vanilla or maple flavoring

Mix sugar, milk, and butter in pan, bring to boil. Remove from heat. Add powdered sugar to make a spreading consistency. Add vanilla or maple flavoring.

Black Forest Torte

Cake
1 cup flour
2 teaspoons baking powder
½ teaspoon salt
⅓ cup cocoa (dry)
3 eggs
1 teaspoon vanilla
1 cup sugar
½ cup boiling water

Other ingredients
1 recipe Butter Cream
1 can cherry pie filling
1½ cups whipping cream *or*
    3 packages whipped
    topping mix
maraschino cherry juice
1 square semi-sweet chocolate

Combine flour, baking powder, salt and cocoa. Stir well to blend and set aside. Beat eggs and vanilla until thick. Add sugar gradually and continue beating. Add dry ingredients with mixer at low speed. Add boiling water. Mix well. Pour batter into 2 large round cake pans. Bake at 400° for 20 minutes. When cool split each layer into two. Place bottom layer on large cake plate. Cover with a layer of Butter Cream, then ⅓ can of cherry pie filling. Continue in this way until all cake layers are used up except one. Whip cream and add 2 tablespoons cherry juice. Spread ¼ of cream on cake, then top with last layer. Cover entire cake with cream. Chill for several hours. At serving time place some maraschino cherries around top of cake and sprinkle with grated chocolate.

Butter Cream: 1 package chocolate pudding mix, 2 cups milk, ⅔ cup soft butter. Cook pudding and cool. Cream butter and beat in cooled pudding. If necessary refrigerate until of spreading consistency.

Very elegant!

Christmas Cake *(very light)*

½ pound butter
1 cup sugar
3 egg yolks
1 teaspoon baking powder
2¾ cups pastry flour
1 cup heated pineapple (juice)
2 teaspoons vanilla
1 pound white raisins
1 pound red cherries
1 pound green cherries
½ pound mixed peel
1½ pounds Brazil nuts, whole
Last add 3 stiffly beaten
    egg whites.

Method: same as for Fruit Cake on page 35.

Fruit Cake *(medium color)*

½ pound butter
2 cups white sugar
4 eggs
2½ cups pastry flour
2 teaspoons baking powder
1 cup sweet milk

Fruit additions
1–2 pounds raisins
½ pound peel
½ pound almonds
½ pound red cherries
¼ pound green cherries
1 cup candied pineapple
2 cups shredded coconut
½ pound gum drops
½ pound dates

Cream butter and sugar, and eggs. Fold in 2 cups flour and baking powder alternately with milk. Add ½ cup flour to coat the fruits.

Bake at 250° for 3–4 hours. Keep pan of water in oven.

Christmas Cake

2 pounds raisins
½ pound glazed cherries
½ pound candied pineapple
    (diced)
1½ pounds dates
1 pound gum drops
1 pound mixed peel
1 pound mixed fruit
½ pound almonds
½ cup corn syrup
1 teaspoon each of cinnamon,
    cloves, nutmeg, allspice, salt
12 eggs, separated
1 pound white sugar
1 pound butter
1 teaspoon soda
3¼ cups flour

Cream butter and sugar. Add egg yolks and corn syrup. Add half of flour to fruit. Add remaining flour, soda and spices. Mix all together. Add stiff egg whites. Bake 2 hours—1 hour at 350°, 1 hour at 300°. Delicious and moist.
Note: Add pan of water to oven while baking.

Spicy and delicious!

Candies

Very Old Fudge

2 cups white sugar
½ cup corn syrup
½ cup milk or cream
butter—size of walnut

Boil slowly—stirring occasionally. Boil until soft to medium ball stage. Cool, add vanilla and beat with a wooden spoon until stiff. Add nuts and cherries, if desired.
For chocolate fudge add 2 tablespoons cocoa to white sugar.

Horehound Candy

¾ cup brewed horehound tea
¼ cup vinegar
2 cups white sugar

Do not stir.
Boil till it cracks in cold water.
Pour into small narrow pan till hardened. This should be as clear as glass and cannot be cut when hard. Must be broken into pieces.

Chocolate Nut Caramels

2 cups white sugar
½ cup corn syrup
2 cups cream
½ cup butter or margarine
6 tablespoons cocoa
1 cup walnuts
2 teaspoons vanilla

Boil together sugar, corn syrup, cocoa, butter and 1 cup cream.
Boil until it threads, then add slowly the other cup cream.
Boil to firm ball stage when tested in cold water.
Add vanilla and nuts, beat till creamy.

Maple Cream Candy

2 cups brown sugar
½ cup cream
butter—size of an egg

Stir all together.
Boil until it drops from spoon.
Add vanilla.
Beat until it thickens.
Pour into buttered pan.

Peanut Butter Fudge

2 cups white sugar
½ cup sweet milk
2 large tablespoons
    peanut butter

Mix well and boil exactly 5 minutes. Beat until thick. Put into buttered pans to cool.

Cracker-Jack

1 small box puffed rice
½ pound blanched peanuts
1 cup corn syrup
1 cup molasses
2 cups brown sugar
1 tablespoon butter
2 tablespoons vinegar
½ teaspoon soda

Boil all ingredients except puffed rice and peanuts until a small amount will form a ball in cold water. Then pour over puffed rice and peanuts and stir till mixed. Form into balls with buttered hands and drop on buttered pans.

Candied Grapefruit

Skin of 2 grapefruit, sliver.
Cover with water, add a dash of salt. Boil for 5 minutes and drain.
Repeat twice more.

Boil 1 cup white sugar, 2 cups water.
Add rinds, boil until syrup is well soaked in.
Add green color if desired. Roll in granulated sugar and store.

Children's Favorite Maple Cream

4 cups brown sugar
2 tablespoons flour
2 teaspoons baking powder
1 cup thin cream
4 tablespoons butter
pinch of salt

Mix ingredients well. Cook, stirring constantly, until mixture forms a soft ball when tried in cold water.
Add chopped pecans or walnuts is desired.
Spread into buttered shallow pan.

Caramel Corn

7 quarts popped corn
2 cups brown sugar
1 cup butter
vanilla
½ cup corn syrup
1 teaspoon salt
½ teaspoon soda

Boil sugar, butter and corn syrup 4 minutes. Remove from stove and add salt, soda and vanilla. (This will foam when soda is added.) Pour over popped corn, stir carefully. Put into a large pan into oven at 250° 1 hour. Carefully stir every 10 minutes. If pan is big enough, shake popcorn—it doesn't crumble as much.

Peanut Brittle

2 cups white sugar
1 cup corn syrup
½ cup water
3 cups salted peanuts
1 teaspoon butter, melted
1 teaspoon soda
1 teaspoon vanilla

Combine sugar and syrup and water. Cook to the hard ball stage. Add peanuts and melted butter and continue cooking until syrup is a golden brown. Stir during cooking. Remove from heat and add soda and vanilla and beat until soda is mixed through syrup. Pour into buttered pans and break into pieces when cold.

Chocolate Fudge

2 cups white sugar
⅔ cup evaporated milk
salt—few grains
¼ cup butter

Boil for 5 minutes, stirring constantly. Start timing when it boils at edge. Add vanilla, 2 cups miniature marshmallows (about 16 large ones cut), 1 package chocolate chips (6 ounces), ½ cup walnut pieces.
Beat until it starts to set.
You may drop each piece and press pecan on top or pour into pan and cut.

Easy Caramels

3 cups white sugar
1 cup corn syrup
1 cup heavy cream
1 cup milk
2 tablespoons cornstarch
4 tablespoons butter
½ teaspoon salt
1 teaspoon vanilla
1 cup nutmeats if desired

Thoroughly mix cornstarch, sugar, corn syrup, milk and cream, butter and salt. Stir mixture over low heat until sugar is dissolved and then cook until mixture is 248° or until a few drops are as hard as caramels should be when finished. Stir only occasionally so mixture will not stick to bottom.
Remove from heat and let cool a few minutes before adding nuts and vanilla.
Pour into buttered pan and when cold cut and wrap in waxed paper.
Caution: Use a heavy saucepan.

Divinity Fudge

1½ cups white sugar
1 cup brown sugar
½ cup corn syrup
¾ cup water
pinch of salt

Cook together until dissolved, then uncover and cook to hard ball stage (265°). Add salt and let stand while you beat 1 egg white. Add 1 teaspoon vanilla and almond flavoring if desired.
Beat until candy stands in peaks.
Drop by teaspoon on waxed paper.

Orange Candy

1 cup white sugar
1½ cups rich milk
2 cups white sugar
grated rind of 2 oranges
¼ teaspoon salt
⅔ cup butter
1 cup nutmeats

Melt first cup of sugar in a large kettle slowly, while milk is scalding in double boiler. When sugar is melted to a rich golden yellow, add milk all at once, stirring. It will boil up quickly so be sure to use a large kettle.

Add the 2 cups sugar to this mixture until dissolved, cook until mixture forms an almost hard ball in cold water. Just before it is finished add grated orange rind, salt, butter and nuts.
Beat till creamy and pour into buttered pan. When cool cut in squares.

Cookies, Squares and Bar Cookies

Oatmeal Raisin Cookies *(drop)*

1¾ cups sifted
   all-purpose flour
1 teaspoon baking powder
1 teaspoon soda
½ teaspoon salt
2 eggs
1¼ cups white sugar
½ cup shortening
   (or part butter and lard)
6 tablespoons molasses
   (Domolco preferred)
1 teaspoon vanilla
2 cups quick oatmeal

Sift flour, baking powder, salt, sugar, soda into mixing bowl. Add unbeaten eggs, shortening, molasses and vanilla. Stir with wooden spoon until smooth (1½ minutes) or beat with mixer until smooth. Then add rolled oats and ½ cup chopped raisins, ⅓ cup chopped walnuts. Drop 4 inches apart on greased cookie sheet. Bake at 325° for 12–15 minutes. Baked cookies should be approximately 2¾ inches in diameter.

Rice Flake Balls *(unbaked)*

In a small pan cook 1 tablespoon butter, 2 eggs, 1 cup sugar, ⅛ teaspoon salt, 1½ pound dates. Use low heat for about 10 minutes. Remove from heat and add 3 cups rice flakes. Shape into balls and roll in coconut.

Melting Moments

Cream 1 cup butter, ¾ cup brown sugar, 1 egg, 1 teaspoon vanilla and add 1¾ cup all-purpose flour sifted and ½ teaspoon cream of tartar and ½ teaspoon soda. Make into little balls. Press a pecan on top of each.

A 'bargain' is something you have to find use for, once you have bought it.

Rolled Oatmeal Cookies (drop)

½ cup butter
½ cup shortening
1 cup brown sugar
2 tablespoons hot water
1 teaspoon soda
2 cups sifted pastry flour
2 cups quick oatmeal
½ teaspoon salt
1 teaspoon vanilla

Cream butter and shortening and sugar until light and fluffy. Add flour and salt and oatmeal. Lastly add soda dissolved in water and vanilla.
Roll very thin, about ⅛ inch thick. Cut with soup can. Bake at 350°.

Date Filling
½ pound dates
½ cup water
2 tablespoons brown sugar
2 tablespoons orange juice
1 tablespoon lemon juice

Chop dates. Simmer ingredients until well blended. Cool and refrigerate. Fill cookies when ready to serve.

Everybody's favorite!

Molasses Krinkles (molded)

2½ cups sifted pastry flour
2 teaspoons soda
½ teaspoon salt
1–2 teaspoons ginger (to taste)
1–2 teaspoons cinnamon
    (to taste)
¾ cup shortening
1 cup white sugar
1 egg, unbeaten
4 tablespoons molasses

Sift flour once, measure; add soda and spices. Sift 3 times. Cream shortening, add sugar and egg. Beat thoroughly. Add molasses, then add flour gradually. Roll in 1¼ inch balls after dough is well chilled and roll in sugar. Bake on ungreased pan 15–20 minutes in 350° oven.

Raisin Ginger Cookies—add 1½ cups raisins

Sugar Cookies *(rolled)*

1 cup shortening
1 cup butter
1 cup white sugar
1 cup brown sugar
4 eggs, well beaten
5 cups all-purpose flour
2 teaspoons soda
4 teaspoons cream of tartar
1 teaspoon salt
2 teaspoons vanilla

Cream shortening and butter and add sugar, creaming thoroughly, then add well beaten eggs and mix again. Add sifted ingredients and vanilla.

Chill dough in refrigerator several hours or overnight. Roll about ⅛ inch thick, sprinkle with sugar. Bake 8 minutes at 350°. Use soup can as cookie cutter (2½ inch diameter).

Ice Cream Cookies: Use above Sugar Cookie recipe and use the following filling to make sandwich cookies: 1 cup sweet cream, 6 tablespoons brown sugar, 1 tablespoon butter, 2 teaspoons vanilla. Boil until thick. Fill cookies while warm. Chill.

Oatmeal Cereal Cookies *(drop)*

¾ cup shortening and
   butter mixed
1 cup brown sugar
1 cup white sugar
2 eggs
1 teaspoon vanilla
2 cups pastry flour
1 teaspoon soda
½ teaspoon baking powder
2 cups quick oatmeal
½ teaspoon salt
1 cup crisp rice cereal
¾ cup coconut

Drop on greased pan and bake at 350°. Baked cookies should be approximately 2¾ inches in diameter.

The only thing that keeps a man going is energy. And what is energy but liking life?

Butter Crunch Cookies

Sift:
1 cup all-purpose flour
¼ teaspoon baking powder
½ teaspoon baking soda

Cream together in order given:
⅔ cup soft butter
1 cup brown sugar
1 egg
1 teaspoon vanilla

Fold together the above
    two mixtures. Then add:
¾ cup oatmeal
1 cup flaked coconut
1 cup corn flakes

Drop in small balls on ungreased cookie sheet. They spread as they bake.
Bake at 350° for 10–12 minutes.
Yield: 3½ dozen

You'll like these!

Cherry Winks

Cream ¾ cup shortening, 1 cup sugar, 2 eggs, 1 teaspoon vanilla.
Sift 2¼ cups all-purpose flour, 1 teaspoon baking powder and ½ teaspoon soda, ½ teaspoon salt.
Mix the creamed mixture and dry ingredients and add 1 cup chopped pecans, 1 cup chopped dates.
Shape into balls. Roll in 2½ cups corn flakes and press half a maraschino cherry into each. Bake at 350–375° 10–12 minutes.

Gratitude is the sign of noble souls.

Oatmeal-Walnut Cookies

Basic Batter
1 cup shortening
1 cup brown sugar
1 cup white sugar
½ teaspoon vanilla
2 eggs
Cream together in order given. Add dry ingredients:
1¼ cups flour
1 teaspoon soda
½ teaspoon cinnamon

Additions suggested:
Option "A"   Fold in 3 cups oatmeal, ½ cup (or more) black walnuts.

Option "B"   Fold in 2 cups oatmeal, 1 cup coconut, 2 cups cornflakes.

Option "C"   Fold in 3 cups oatmeal, ½ cup chopped walnuts and omit the spices.

Drop by teaspoon on greased cookie sheet. Bake at 350–375° for 10–15 minutes.

Quickest Easiest Oatmeal Cookies

Into a mixing bowl sift:
2 cups pastry flour
1 teaspoon cinnamon
1 teaspoon soda
½ teaspoon salt
Add:
2 cups oatmeal
Make a hole in the center.

In a small pan bring to
    boiling point:
1 cup brown sugar
Add:
1 cup corn oil
⅓ cup water

Mix the warm mixture into the dry ingredients. Drop by spoonful on greased cookie sheet, while the dough is still warm. Bake at 350–375° 10–15 minutes.

Peppermint Cookies with Milk

Bring to boil 1 cup milk.
Dissolve 2 tablespoons baking ammonia or baking powder in hot milk.
Add 1 cup shortening and stir to dissolve.
Add 12 drops oil of peppermint and
1 cup cold milk.
Stir this liquid into mixture of
9 cups all-purpose flour
2½ cups sugar
(Dough should be soft.)
Refrigerate for a few hours.
Roll dough ¼ inch thick and cut with cookie cutter. Bake at 375° until light

Refreshing!

Unbaked Chocolate Roll

Mix together:
1 egg, slightly beaten
1 cup powdered sugar
1 cup graham wafer crumbs
2 squares chocolate melted with
    2 tablespoons butter
½ cup chopped walnuts
1 cup miniature marshmallows

Shape into roll on waxed paper.
Roll in coconut and chill until ready to serve.
Cut into slices to serve.

Cornflake Drops

Mix together:
¼ cup butter
1 cup brown sugar
2 eggs, beaten
¼ teaspoon vanilla
1 teaspoon almond flavoring

Sift together:
2 cups flour
2 teaspoons baking powder

Add to creamed mixture. Add 4 cups
cornflakes. Drop by teaspoonful onto greased
cookie sheet.
Bake at 350° for 12–15 minutes.

Marmalade Nut Cookies

Mix together:
½ cup butter or margarine
⅔ cup brown sugar
1 egg
1 teaspoon vanilla

Sift together:
1¾ cups all-purpose flour
2 teaspoons baking powder
½ teaspoon salt
½ teaspoon soda

Stir into first mixture and add:
1 cup chopped walnuts
½ cup marmalade

Drop on greased cookie sheet and bake at 350° for 10–12 minutes.

Tempters

½ cup shortening
1 cup white sugar
1 beaten egg
1 teaspoon vanilla
¼ teaspoon almond extract
2 tablespoons milk
2 cups pastry flour
    (1¾ cups all-purpose)
1½ teaspoons baking powder
½ teaspoon salt
½ cup nuts (optional)
½ cup chocolate chips
1 cup coconut

Cream shortening, blend in sugar, egg, flavorings and milk. Mix in dry ingredients ⅓ at a time. Mix in nuts, etc. Drop by teaspoonful on greased cookie sheet. Press with wet fork. Bake at 350° about 12 minutes.

Cornflake Macaroons

Beat 3 egg whites until stiff. Gradually add 1½ cups sugar and 1 teaspoon vanilla. Fold in 3 cups cornflakes and ½ cup coconut.
Baking method same as for Coconut Kisses (page 52).

Walnut Logs

1 cup walnuts
½ cup dates
¾ cup desiccated coconut
1 egg, slightly beaten

Grind or cut finely dates and nuts. Mix in the beaten egg and the coconut. Shape into logs ¾x1 inch and roll them in extra coconut (about ¼ cup).
Bake at 350° 10–15 minutes.

Shortbreads *(They melt in your mouth.)*

No. 1 Using the electric beater, cream until very light 1 pound butter, while still beating add ½ cup brown sugar and ½ cup powdered sugar, 1 teaspoon vanilla and ⅛ teaspoon salt. Beat 5 minutes. Add 4 cups all-purpose flour using beater at first and hands last. The heat of the hands helps the process! These may be pressed into shapes from a press or they may be chilled a bit and then rolled and cut into shapes. Decorate. Bake at 325° about 7 minutes.
Yield: 75 cookies

No. 2 Oatmeal Shortbread
Cream very well in order given:
1 cup butter, ½ cup brown sugar, ½ cup powdered sugar, ½ teaspoon vanilla.
Add 1½ cups oatmeal and then 1 cup all-purpose flour sifted with 1 teaspoon baking powder. May be made into small balls and flattened. May be made into roll about 8 inches long and 1½ inches in diameter, then rolled in chocolate shot, chilled and sliced. Bake at 325° 7–10 minutes.
Yield: 75 cookies

No. 3 Almond or Filbert Shortbread
Use the same recipe as No. 1 or No. 2 and add ½–1 cup crushed almonds or filberts.
Yield: 75 cookies

Coconut Kisses

Beat ½ cup egg whites until stiff. Gradually add 1¼ cups sugar, ½ teaspoon salt, ½ teaspoon vanilla. Fold in 2½ cups moist coconut.
Drop by spoonful on ungreased brown paper which rests on an ungreased cookie sheet. Bake at 325° about 20 minutes—light golden.
Slide the paper onto a wet towel to rest for a minute before removing cookies.

Health Cookies

¾ cup shortening
1½ cups brown sugar
1 egg
½ cup water
1 teaspoon vanilla
1 cup flour
1 teaspoon salt
½ teaspoon soda
1 cup powdered milk
2 cups oatmeal (uncooked)
1 cup wheat germ

Cream all the wet ingredients with mixer. Add sifted flour, salt and soda. Blend in the milk, oats and wheat germ.

These are good plain with an almond sliver on top. You may add any combination of the following: raisins, dates, coconut, or chocolate chips.

Drop by spoonful on greased cookie sheet. Bake at 350° 12–15 minutes.

Fruit Jumbos

1 cup white sugar
½ cup butter
1 teaspoon soda dissolved in
    2 tablespoons hot water
2 eggs
1 teaspoon vanilla
2 cups all-purpose flour

Cream the sugar, butter, soda and eggs and vanilla with beater. Fold in the flour.
Add the following:
1 cup walnuts
1 pound dates (or 1 cup dates and ½ cup peel)
½ pound green cherries
½ pound red cherries

Bake at 350° 10–12 minutes.

Chocolate Swirls (unbaked)

Mix in order given:
2 cups powdered sugar
3 tablespoons water
½ cup dried milk powder
1 teaspoon vanilla
3 cups coconut

Melt 6 ounces chocolate or butterscotch chips over warm water.

Drop cookies on wax paper and after they have stood 10 minutes swirl chocolate over tops.

Cherry Surprises *(unbaked)*

Beat together:
½ cup soft butter
1¼ cups sifted powdered sugar
1 tablespoon orange juice
1½ cups desiccated coconut

You will need about 3½ dozen maraschino cherries to make the centers.

Make cookies by putting batter around a cherry and then rolling each in graham cracker crumbs.

Coconut or Chocolate Clusters *(unbaked) Look and taste like a candy.*

½ cup peanut butter
1 cup powdered sugar
½ cup fine nuts
½ cup coconut
1 cup chopped dates
1 tablespoon butter
1 teaspoon vanilla

Mix together. Form into balls. Roll in coconut, or roll in melted chocolate mixture of 8 ounces unsweetened or semi-sweet chocolate with ¼ cup paraffin wax.

Those dipped in chocolate should be stored in the refrigerator.

Yum! Yum! Better as they age!

Brownies

2 squares chocolate
½ cup butter
1 cup sugar
2 eggs
½ cup flour
½ teaspoon salt
1 teaspoon vanilla
½ cup nuts

Cream butter and sugar, add eggs and beat well. Add dry ingredients, melted chocolate, vanilla, nuts. Bake at 350° for 35 minutes.

Let there be spaces in your togetherness.

Apple Blossom Cookies

a)   Cream together ½ cup shortening, 1 cup sugar, and 2 eggs, 2 tablespoons cream and 1 teaspoon vanilla. Sift together 2 cups all-purpose flour, 1 teaspoon baking powder and ½ teaspoon salt. Sift into the creamed mix using hands at the last. Chill. Roll to ⅛ inch thickness and cut 1½–2 inches rounds. Bake at 350° about 10 minutes to a light color.

b)   To a 3 ounce package of raspberry gelatin powder, add ½ cup boiling water and set aside in a warm place to use later.

c)   In the top of double boiler add 2 egg whites, 1½ cups sugar, 5 tablespoons water, 1 tablespoon corn syrup, and a pinch of salt. Beat with a rotary beater for about 7 minutes. There should be a stiff icing with sharp peaks. Stir in the gelatin mix now and beat well again. Cool, stirring occasionally. It is a marshmallow texture.

d)   Drop a small spoonful of raspberry jelly on each cookie and then a spoonful of the marshmallow mix on top of that. The edge of the cookie should show evenly.

e)   Turn each cookie upside down and dip into coconut while the mixture is still moist. They are pretty and delicious. Yield: 5 dozen

Strawberry Cookies (unbaked)

Mix together:
1 can sweetened condensed milk
½ package strawberry gelatin
1 heaping tablespoon powdered sugar
2 cups fine coconut
½ cup almonds, finely chopped or ground

Chill overnight.

Shape into berry shapes and roll in remaining gelatin powder.
Attach small leaves of green colored icing.

Fancy! For the tea plate.

Only he who attempts the ridiculous can achieve the impossible.

Mint Chocolate Sticks

Make brownies (use your favorite recipe or the one on page 54) and spread filling over top.

Filling

Work 2 tablespoons soft butter into 1 cup sifted powdered sugar. Add 1 tablespoon cream, ¾ teaspoon peppermint. Stir until smooth. Keep filling-covered cake in fridge while making the glaze.

Glaze

Melt together 1 square unsweetened chocolate and 1 tablespoon butter. Drizzle over cool, firm filling. Tilt cake back and forth until glaze covers surface. Refrigerate. Cut into strips 2½x¾ inches.

Pecan Fingers

1 cup dark brown sugar
1 cup soft butter
1 egg
½ teaspoon vanilla
2 cups sifted all-purpose flour
1 egg, well beaten
½ cup dark brown sugar
1 cup coarsely chopped pecans
½ cup dark brown sugar

Heat oven to 350°. Lightly grease a jelly-roll pan 15x10x1 inches.
Combine 1 cup sugar and butter and cream until fluffy. Add 1 egg and vanilla and beat until well blended.
Add flour and work into creamed mixture until well blended. Spread in prepared pan. Brush with beaten egg.
Sprinkle with ½ cup sugar, then with nuts and then with remaining sugar, spreading evenly over top. Bake 20–25 minutes or until nicely browned. Cool in pan and cut in fingers to serve.
Note: Dark brown sugar gives the best flavor in this recipe but any brown sugar will be satisfactory.

Chocolate Marshmallow Squares

Make Brownies (page 54). When still hot cut 24 marshmallows in half (miniature may be used) and place on top of baked brownies, place in oven 3 minutes. Cool and frost with 1 square unsweetened chocolate.

Apple Squares

2½ cups all-purpose flour
1 or 2 tablespoons sugar
1 teaspoon salt
1 cup shortening

Mix as for pie crust. In a cup put one egg and add enough milk to make ⅔ cup. Mix all together. Roll half of dough on cookie sheet, on top of rolled dough sprinkle 6 handfuls of cornflakes crushed. (Use more or less according to apples.) Now put a layer of apples which have been peeled and diced.
Add a cup of sugar and 1 teaspoon of cinnamon. Roll rest of dough and put on top. Bake about 20 to 30 minutes, and ice immediately with a glaze: 1 cup powdered sugar, vanilla, 3 tablespoons water.
(Do not cover tightly to store.)

Custard Cream Bars (unbaked)

½ cup butter
¼ cup sugar
5 tablespoons cocoa
1 teaspoon vanilla
2 eggs
2 cups graham wafer crumbs
1 cup coconut
½ cup walnuts

Place softened butter, sugar, cocoa, vanilla and eggs in top of double boiler. Mix well and set over boiling water. Stir until the mixture resembles custard. Combine wafer crumbs, coconut and nuts. Add cooked mixture. Pack evenly in a 9 inch greased square pan. Frost with the following.

Icing
Cream ¼ cup butter, add 3 tablespoons milk combined with 2 tablespoons vanilla custard powder. Blend in 2 cups sifted powdered sugar.
Spread over chocolate base and let stand 15 minutes. Melt 4 squares semi-sweet chocolate with 1 tablespoon butter and spread over the custard icing. When set cut into bars.

Charming Cherry Bars

1 cup flour
¼ cup powdered sugar *or*
    2 tablespoons brown sugar
½ cup butter
Mix all together. Press in 9x9 inch pan and bake for 10 minutes at 350°.

Sift together:
¼ cup flour
½ teaspoon baking powder
¼ teaspoon salt
1 cup brown sugar
Add 2 eggs (slightly beaten)
Fold in ½ cup maraschino cherries (cut up)
½ cup shredded coconut
½ cup walnuts
Spread over partially baked dough. Return to oven and bake 25 minutes.

Icing
1 cup brown sugar
¼ cup table cream
1 tablespoon butter
Boil 2 minutes. Let cool. Add powdered sugar to thicken.

Rocky Road Squares

½ cup butter or margarine
1 cup powdered sugar
1 6-ounce package
    butterscotch chips
1 beaten egg

Heat in double boiler until melted. Then cool slightly. Add 2 cups miniature marshmallows. Pour into 8x8 inch pan lined with whole graham wafers. Then refrigerate.

There is no place more delightful than home.

Raspberry Squares

1 cup flour
1 teaspoon baking powder
⅛ teaspoon salt
½ cup butter
1 tablespoon milk
1 egg, beaten

Mix like pie dough. Roll and put in pan. Spread on raspberry jam in thin layer.

Then mix:
1 cup white sugar
1 beaten egg
¼ cup melted butter
2 cups coconut
1 teaspoon vanilla

Mix well and spread over jam. Bake in moderate oven 25 minutes.

"O Henry" Squares

1 cup brown sugar
½ cup butter
½ cup milk
Add:
1 cup crushed graham wafers
1 cup walnuts
1 cup coconut
1 cup finely chopped cherries

Place 9 wafers in 8x8 inch pan, pour mixture on top. Put 9 graham wafers on top of mixture. Ice with butter icing.

Fruit Squares

2 eggs
½ cup margarine
¾ cup sugar
¼ teaspoon salt
1 teaspoon baking powder
¾ cup flour
½ cup chopped raisins
½ cup chopped dates
1 teaspoon vanilla

Pour into well greased 9x12 inch pan. Bake at 325° for 30 minutes. When cool, ice with powdered sugar. Cut in squares.

Marshmallow Delights (unbaked)

½ cup butter
¾ cup brown sugar
½ cup chopped walnuts
2 eggs, beaten
¼ cup coconut
3 cups miniature marshmallows (colored)
2½ cups graham wafer crumbs

Melt butter in top of double boiler. Add eggs, sugar, and coconut and set over simmering water. Cool to lukewarm.
Blend in crumbs, nuts and marshmallows.
Pack into buttered pan 12x8x2 inches.
Ice with butter icing. Cut in squares.
Can be used without icing if preferred.

Caramel Krisp (unbaked)

7 ounce package caramels
2 tablespoons water in double boiler
Melt over hot water.
½ cup nuts
pinch of salt
Put in with caramels when all is melted.
Add:
7 cups cornflakes or crisp rice cereal
Put on greased cookie sheet. Let set till cool.

Cookies, Squares and Bar Cookies

Tropical Bars

1 cup sifted all-purpose flour
¼ teaspoon salt
¼ cup brown sugar, packed
¼ cup butter
1 egg
1 cup brown sugar, packed
1 teaspoon rum extract
½ cup sifted all-purpose flour
½ teaspoon baking powder
¼ teaspoon salt
1 cup flaked coconut
¼ cup cut-up
   maraschino cherries
½ cup well drained
   crushed pineapple

Heat oven to 350°. Lightly grease a 9 inch square cake pan.
Sift 1 cup flour and ¼ teaspoon salt into bowl. Add ¼ cup brown sugar and blend lightly. Add butter and work into dry ingredients first with a fork and then with fingers until mixture is crumbly. Press firmly into bottom of prepared pan. Bake 15 minutes. Remove from oven. Beat egg thoroughly. Add 1 cup brown sugar gradually, beating well after each addition. Beat in rum extract.
Sift ½ cup flour, baking powder and ¼ teaspoon salt into mixture and stir to blend. Stir in coconut, cherries and pineapple. Spread over hot pastry layer and return to oven. Bake about 35 minutes or until well browned. Cool in pan and cut in bars.

Butter Nut Chews

½ cup brown sugar (packed)
½ cup shortening (half butter)
1 cup sifted all-purpose flour
2 eggs, well beaten
½ cup brown sugar
½ cup corn syrup
1 teaspoon vanilla
1 tablespoon flour
½ teaspoon salt
½ teaspoon baking powder
1 cup coconut
1 cup walnuts *or* pecans

Mix first three ingredients to form crumbs and press into a 9x9x2 inch pan (ungreased). Bake at 350° for 10 minutes.
Mix remaining ingredients in order given, spread over crumbs and return to oven and bake for 25 minutes longer or until golden brown.
Makes 24 bars.

Oatmeal Squares

¼ pound butter
¾ cup brown sugar
1¾ cups rolled oats

Melt butter on stove, add sugar and bring to a boil. Take off stove and add oats. Spread in square pan. Bake in very slow oven 10 minutes.

Graham Wafer Squares

15 double graham wafers
    broken into chunks
½ pound cut marshmallows
½ cup cut dates
½ cup chopped walnuts
Mix.
Put into saucepan:
1 cup water
½ cup margarine
2 eggs
3 tablespoons cocoa
Boil 1 minute.

Mix into first ingredients and press into greased 8x10 inch pan. Put into refrigerator to set, ice with a chocolate icing.

Magic Cookie Bars

½ cup butter
1½ cups graham wafer crumbs
1 cup chopped walnuts
6 ounces chocolate chips
1½ cups coconut
15 ounces sweetened
    condensed milk

First melt butter and put in bottom of pan. Then graham wafers, walnuts, chocolate chips, coconut, each a layer at a time. Don't bother stirring. Last pour sweetened condensed milk on top. Bake till brown at 350°. Leave set 15 minutes, then cut in bars.

Old Fashioned Raisin Bars

1 cup seedless raisins
1 cup water
½ cup salad oil
1 cup sugar
1 slightly beaten egg
1¾ cups flour
¼ teaspoon salt
1 teaspoon soda
1 teaspoon cinnamon
½ teaspoon nutmeg
½ teaspoon allspice
1 teaspoon cloves
½ cup walnuts

Combine raisins and water, bring to boiling, remove from heat. Stir in salad oil. Cool to lukewarm.
Stir in sugar and egg.
Sift together dry ingredients, beat into raisin mixture. Stir in nuts.
Pour into greased 13x9x2 inch pan. Bake at 375° for 20 minutes. When cool cut in bars. Dust with confectioners sugar.

Lemon Squares

Crumbs
1 cup soda cracker crumbs
½ cup butter
1 cup brown sugar
1 cup coconut
½ teaspoon baking soda
1 cup flour

Press ¾ of crumbs in bottom of 9x9 inch pan. Bake 25 minutes in slow oven (325°). Add filling and remaining crumbs sprinkled on top. Bake 20 minutes longer.

Filling
1 cup white sugar
2 tablespoons cornstarch (rounded)
2 eggs, slightly beaten
1 cup cold water
¼ cup butter (melted)
½ teaspoon vanilla
1 lemon and rind

Date Pinwheels

½ cup butter
½ cup brown sugar
½ cup white sugar
1 egg
½ teaspoon vanilla
2 cups pastry flour
⅛ teaspoon salt
¼ teaspoon soda

Cream butter, add sugars, egg and vanilla in order given. Add sifted flour, salt and soda. Chill until firm enough to roll.

Make date filling:
Cut 7–8 ounces dates, add ⅓ cup water, ¼ cup sugar, ⅛ teaspoon salt. Simmer 5 minutes. Stir often. Add 1 cup nuts. Cool.
Option: add grated rind of 1 lemon and 1 tablespoon lemon juice.

Roll cookie dough to 9x12 inches. Spread with cooled date mixture. Roll up tightly and wrap in wax paper and chill or freeze overnight for easier slicing. Slice ⅛ inch thick. Bake on greased cookie sheet 350–375° for 10 minutes. Store in airtight container.

Rolls may be kept in freezer and sliced for baking as needed.

Butterscotch Squares

¼ cup butter
1 cup brown sugar
1 egg
1 cup flour
1 teaspoon baking powder
¼ teaspoon salt
½ cup chopped nuts
1 teaspoon vanilla

Melt butter and add to sugar, add egg and mix well. Sift dry ingredients and mix with first mixture. Add nuts and vanilla. Spread into greased 8x8 inch pan. Bake at 350° for 30 minutes. Cut into squares or bars while warm.

Date Oatmeal Squares

¾ cup shortening
¾ cup brown sugar
1¾ cups all-purpose flour
1½ cups oatmeal
½ teaspoon soda
½ cup chopped walnuts
   (optional)

Filling
½ pound dates
¼ cup corn syrup
½ cup water
1 tablespoon lemon juice

Cook filling till thickened, then cool.
Mix flour, oatmeal, soda, nuts and
brown sugar.
Add shortening and mix thoroughly. Put half
of mixture in pan. Spread the cool date
mixture over this and top with remaining
oatmeal mixture.
Pat down. Bake at 350° for 30 minutes.

Jam Squares: 1 cup raspberry jam in place
of date filling. Add 2 teaspoons lemon rind to
crumb mixture. Very good.

Casseroles and Supper Dishes

Delicious Chicken Casserole

1 cup uncooked rice
1 can cream of mushroom
   soup undiluted
1 cup water
1 package dry onion soup mix
6 chicken legs or 4 breasts or
   1 chicken

Mix rice, soups and water together in a large casserole and lay chicken pieces on top and cover tightly. Bake at 325° for 2 hours or more. Do not peek!

Chicken with Rice Casserole

1 3-pound chicken cut up, or
   legs or breasts uncooked
1 cup uncooked rice
4 cups hot water
1 package onion soup mix
1 can mushroom soup
1 package chicken with
   rice soup mix *or*
     1 tablespoon chicken broth
   concentrate

In bottom of oblong casserole put rice, then chicken pieces. The soup mixes dissolved in the 4 cups hot water poured over top. Paprika if desired over top. Bake at 350° for 2 hours.

Tuna Noodle Casserole

1 chopped onion
1 tablespoon butter
1 can cream of mushroom
   soup
½ cup milk
1 7-ounce can tuna, drained
1 cup cooked noodles
½ cup drained cooked peas
½ cup shredded cheddar
   cheese

Cook onion in butter until browned. Combine with soup, milk, tuna, noodles and peas. Pour into a 1 quart casserole and top with ½ cup cheese. Bake uncovered for 25 minutes until hot and bubbling at 375°.

Tuna Casserole

½ package noodles, boiled 3
    minutes, drained
    and rinsed
1 can mushroom soup
1 can flaked tuna
½ cup rolled potato chips

Mix noodles, soup and tuna and place in casserole. Sprinkle top with potato chips and dot with butter. Bake in oven at 350° about 45 minutes. Serves 4.

Turkey Pie with English Pastry

3 or 4 cups cut up cooked
    turkey
2 large potatoes, cubed
2 carrots, sliced
1 package frozen peas
1 onion, chopped
leftover gravy made from
    broth that turkey was
    cooked in
cream of chicken or
    mushroom soup

Put legs, thighs, or wings in large pan with water to cover and simmer until done. Take turkey out and remove from bones. To the pot add cut up vegetables and cook until done. Add peas and pieces of turkey meat, season with salt and pepper and cook until peas are done, adding more water if necessary. Mix in gravy and soup. Put in 2-quart casserole lined with English Pastry (recipe below). Put on top crust in which slits have been made. Bake 25 minutes in
425° oven.

English Pastry

2 cups flour
2 teaspoons baking powder
1 teaspoon salt
⅔ cup shortening
½ cup hot water
1 tablespoon lemon juice
1 unbeaten egg yolk

Sift together flour, baking powder, and salt. Mix shortening with hot water, lemon juice and egg yolk. Stir into dry ingredients. Chill dough for easier handling. Use ¾ of dough for lining and remainder for top of Turkey Pie (above).

Beef-Macaroni Dinner

1 package Kraft
  Cheese-and-Macaroni
  Dinner, cooked as directed
  on package
1 can mushroom soup
1 can corn niblets
1 can mushrooms (if desired)
2 cups diced celery
1 can tomato soup
1 small can tomato sauce
1½ pounds ground beef
2 large onions, sliced
2 tablespoons butter

Brown meat and onion in butter in frying pan. Mix all together and season with salt and pepper and dash of Worcestershire sauce. Heat in 325° oven until warm.

Chow Mein

2 pounds hamburger (browned) or 4 cups leftover turkey, chicken or pork
½ cup onions, diced
½ cup celery, diced
Saute onions and celery, then add meat and put in *large* casserole.
Add and mix:
1 can mushroom soup (10 ounces)
1 can mushrooms (10 ounces)
1 can drained bean sprouts (10 ounces)
Top with one box Chinese noodles.
Serves 10–12. Bake until it bubbles.
This is nice for a luncheon with a jellied salad, a tossed salad and French bread.

Remember the steam kettle—
although up to its neck in hot water,
it continues to sing.

A Quickie

1 pound hamburger
diced onion
1 can creamed corn
1 package instant
    mashed potatoes

Brown hamburger with onion until red color disappears. Mix with corn and put in casserole and top with instant mashed potatoes prepared as instructed on package. Bake in oven until you have your salad ready and your table set for dinner, about 20 minutes.

Seven Layer Dinner

1 to 2 inch layer of
    raw sliced potatoes
1 layer sliced raw onions
1 layer sliced raw carrots
¼ cup quick-cooking rice
1 can peas and their liquid
1 pound link style pork
    sausages
1 10-ounce can tomato soup
1 can water
salt and pepper

In a deep greased casserole arrange layer over layer. Salt and pepper each layer. Cover and bake 1 hour at 350°. Uncover and bake 15–30 minutes longer.

1½ pounds ground beef can be substituted for pork sausages.
Going out? Put this in the oven.

Hamburger Tomato Casserole

1 pound hamburger
1 quart canned tomatoes
¾ cup uncooked rice
salt and pepper to taste
cheese slices for top

Combine hamburger, tomatoes and rice. Pour into casserole and bake for approximately 1½ hours at 350°. About ½ hour before serving top with cheese slices and return to oven to finish cooking.

Before working in the garden, rub your fingernails over a piece of soap. Dirt can't get in, and soap washes out easily when washing.

Porcupines

1 pound hamburger
4 slices bread
1 egg
1 cup milk
1 onion
¼ cup uncooked rice
2 cups tomato juice

Crumble bread and soak in milk. Add beaten egg. Mix with other ingredients (except tomato juice). Shape into balls and place in casserole. Pour tomato juice over balls and bake 1½ hours in 350° oven.

Sauerkraut and Pork

Cook fresh pork in lots of water. Add sauerkraut and simmer slowly for about 3 hours.

Some people like to add dumplings at the last and serve immediately when they have cooked 10–12 minutes.

It's the long slow cooking of kraut and pork that makes it good.

Bar-B-Que Burgers

1 pound ground beef
2 tablespoons fat
1 can chicken gumbo soup
½ cup water
1 tablespoon prepared
   mustard
½ cup chopped onion
½ teaspoon salt
⅛ teaspoon pepper
1 tablespoon catsup

Cook meat and onion in hot fat until meat is browned. Stir in remaining ingredients and simmer over low heat 30 minutes. Spoon it from skillet to buns. Makes about 8 hamburgers.

Note: Pour off some of the fat after the meat is partly cooked.

Country-Style Lasagna

1½ pounds hamburger
1 large onion
salt and pepper
½ teaspoon garlic salt
1 teaspoon parsley flakes
2 teaspoons oregano
1 bay leaf, crushed

Cheese Sauce
4 tablespoons shortening
½ teaspoon salt
2 cups milk
4 tablespoons flour
small onion, chopped
1 cup old cheese, grated

Add onions and seasonings to the meat as you brown it, add enough oil to cover pan bottom, take off grease after hamburger is brown. Then add to hamburger 1 quart tomatoes (or 20 ounce can tomatoes add 1 teaspoon sugar), 1 large can tomato paste (11 ounce). Simmer 45 minutes.

Put milk and cheese in pot with other ingredients and stir until cheese sauce is thick.

10 wide noodles or twice what will cover broiler pan. Cook noodles in a large steamer for 14 minutes, stirring as they cook. Put in a sieve, add a little oil, then rinse with cold water. Add a little oil to bottom of pan. Then fill: 1 layer of noodles, half of meat sauce, all of cheese sauce, 2 layers of noodles, then the rest of the meat on top. Put mozzarella cheese over all. Can be left or baked right away at 250° for 1 hour covered with foil. This is a good dish for hungry snowmobilers.

Wiener Casserole

3 large potatoes
1 pound wieners
salt and pepper to taste
1 tablespoon flour
½ cup grated cheese
1 onion, sliced
1 can cream of chicken soup *or*
    1 can cream of mushroom
    soup
sliced tomatoes

Slice potatoes in bottom of casserole. Add seasonings and flour. Cut wieners in ½ inch pieces and add to dish. Sprinkle with cheese and add onion. Pour soup over all and top with sliced tomatoes. (Sprinkle with more grated cheese if desired.) Bake at 350° for 1½ hours.
Serves 4.

Spinach Pie

1 package spinach
6 raw potatoes
3 eggs
1 onion
4 tablespoons melted butter
1 teaspoon salt
pepper

Chop raw spinach very fine. Grate potatoes and add the beaten eggs to avoid discoloration. Grate in onion. Add melted butter and seasoning. Place half of potato mixture into greased baking dish. Pack in spinach. Cover with remaining potato mixture. Bake at 350° for about 30 minutes.
Serves 6. Energy food.

Frankfurter Cheese Boats

1 10-ounce can cream of
  mushroom soup
½ cup milk
2 packages frozen green beans,
  cooked and drained
8 frankfurters
4 slices cheese, cut in strips
4 slices partially cooked bacon,
  cut in half

In shallow (12x8x2 inch) pan stir soup until smooth, gradually blend in milk. Stir in beans. Slit frankfurters lengthwise to about ½ inch from each end. Stuff with cheese. Arrange wieners on beans; top with bacon. Bake at 350° for 25 minutes or until hot.

Big Catch Casserole

1 10-ounce can
  cream of celery soup
½ cup salad dressing
¼ cup milk
¼ cup grated cheese
1 12-ounce package frozen
  peas *or* 1 can peas, juice
  included
1 7½-ounce can salmon *or*
  tuna
4 ounces (2 cups) noodles,
  cooked
1 tablespoon chopped onion

Heat oven to 350°. Cook noodles in salted water and drain. Combine soup, salad dressing, milk and cheese. Blend well. Add peas, salmon, onion, noodles and mix lightly. Pour into 1½ quart casserole. Bake 25 minutes. Serve with salad and rolls.

Corn Casserole

2½ cups corn (cooked or raw)
⅓ cup celery, cut fine
1¼ cups cracker crumbs
½ cup diced cheese
1⅔ cups milk
½ onion, chopped
3 tablespoons melted butter
½ teaspoon salt
3 eggs, separated

Beat egg yolks with milk; add all other ingredients except egg whites. Beat egg whites until stiff and fold in last. Put in a greased casserole or baking dish and top with a bit of bread or cracker crumbs and sprinkle with paprika. Bake ¾–1 hour at 350°.

Super Eggs on Toast

Cook 2 tablespoons finely minced onion in 2 tablespoons butter. Add 1 can cream of celery soup and ⅓ cup milk and heat, stirring until combined.

Meanwhile, poach 6 eggs and toast 6 slices of bread. Place a slice of process cheese on each slice of toast. When ready to serve put under broiler until cheese is melted. Top with poached egg and sauce made with soup.

Pickled Chicken Gizzards

1 pound chicken gizzards
2 cups water
pickling spice
salt
1 onion
approximately 1 cup vinegar

Cover gizzards with water and add about 1 teaspoon salt and teaspoon pickling spice. Cook for 3 hours until very tender. Drain, reserve stock for use in soup or gravies. Place cooked gizzards in 1 quart jar alternating layers of meat with slices of onion. Pour vinegar over and fill jar with cold water. Refrigerate for 24 hours.

The secret of all egg cooking is—
low temperature.

Salmon Patties

One small onion cut fine and
    sauteed to a golden yellow
    in a bit of butter
    (2–3 tablespoons)
Add 2 cups flaked and
    boned salmon
¾ cup coarse cracker crumbs
1 egg, slightly beaten
½ cup milk

Spoon into well buttered skillet and fry a golden brown. Turn and fry other side.

Cabbage Rolls

1 very large head Savoy or
    regular cabbage
2 pounds ground chuck (beef)
1 pound ground pork
½ teaspoon pepper
2 teaspoons salt
1 teaspoon dry mustard
½ cup chopped onion
¼ cup catsup
1 20-ounce can tomato soup
1 48-ounce can tomato juice
½ cup long grain *raw* rice

Remove the core from cabbage and separate leaves carefully. Pour boiling water over leaves and let stand about 2 minutes. Drain leaves very well for about 20 minutes. Mix well all ingredients except tomato soup and juice. Form meatballs about the size of a large egg and put in the center of cabbage leaf and roll up tightly. Place cabbage rolls, open side down, in roasting pan in neat layers. Mix tomato soup and juice well and pour over top. Cover and simmer in oven at 300° for *4 hours.*

Variation: If you enjoy sauerkraut, cabbage rolls may also be placed on a bed of sauerkraut before tomato mixture is poured over. Serve with hot crusty bread.

Cheese Souffle

1½ cups milk
2 cups soft bread crumbs
1½ cups grated cheese
1 tablespoon butter
⅛ teaspoon paprika
1 teaspoon salt
3 eggs, separated

Heat first six ingredients in top of double boiler until cheese is melted. Cool slightly. Add to well beaten egg yolks. Beat egg whites until stiff. Fold cheese and egg mixture into stiffly beaten egg whites. Pour into a well buttered 1½ quart casserole. Place into a pan of hot water and bake at 350° for 40–50 minutes.

Note: Minced chicken, ham, turkey or a 7½-ounce can of salmon may be used instead of cheese.

Cheese and Bread Casserole

2 cups soft bread crumbs
strong yellow cheese thinly sliced or grated
Put crumbs and cheese in a greased casserole in layers until dish is filled.
Beat together: 3 eggs, 1 teaspoon salt, 2 cups scalded milk.
Pour over crumbs and cheese. Milk should fill dish. Bake at 350° until golden brown. (Good with a jellied salad.)

Sweet and Sour Pigtails or Spareribs

Sauce
¼ cup brown sugar
3 tablespoons cornstarch
¼ teaspoon dry mustard
⅛ teaspoon ginger
1 teaspoon salt
¾ teaspoon chili powder
1 clove garlic
5 tablespoons vinegar
1 cup tomato juice
1 cup water
1 teaspoon soy sauce

Mix all ingredients and cook until thickened, stirring frequently. Pour over pigtails or ribs in roast pan. Bake in oven 1 hour. Then add mushrooms, green pepper and red pepper if desired, and bake 1 more hour.

Piggy Casserole

4 cups cooked diced potatoes
5 cups cubed bread
2 pounds ground pork
1½ cups milk
2 eggs
2 tablespoons salt
1 teaspoon black pepper

Cook potatoes with jackets and then peel and cube. Mix with bread and ground pork which should be broken into small pieces. Add milk and eggs, salt and pepper, then bake in casserole for about 1½ hours at 325° or until nicely browned.

Baked Beans (1970 version)

Fry 4 pieces diced bacon in
    small roaster
Add:
1 can or more pork and beans
1 can lima beans (drained)
1 can kidney beans
½ cup vinegar
½ cup sugar
¼ cup molasses
1 diced onion

Bake at 325° for 2–3 hours. (It can be done at a higher heat if you want to use it sooner.) Take this dish to a pot luck dinner or a picnic and the dish is always empty.

Pork and Beans

5 pounds white beans which
    have been soaked overnight
½ teaspoon nutmeg
½ teaspoon pepper
½ teaspoon mustard
4 tablespoons molasses
2 tablespoons salt
2 pounds diced bacon *or*
    1 ham bone

Let this come to a boil until beans are tender. Add ketchup to suit taste and simmer 10 to 15 minutes. If canning, steam pints 15 minutes and quarts 30 minutes. Instead of bacon you can use 1 ham bone which can be removed when beans are cooked.

Fresh Red Beets as a Vegetable

2 cups shredded beets

Add 1 tablespoon butter to heavy pan. Add beets, ½ teaspoon salt. Cook over medium heat stirring occasionally. If beets are young, this takes only about 10 minutes after they are hot. Serves 6.

Hot Cabbage

Cook about 1 quart cabbage in 2 cups boiling water and teaspoon salt for 7 minutes. Drain. Add 1 tablespoon butter and serve.

Sweet and Sour Cabbage

To above cooked Hot Cabbage add:

2 tablespoons vinegar, 2 tablespoons sugar, 3–4 tablespoons sweet or sour cream.

Carrot Potato Chowder

2 cups scalded milk
1 onion, sliced
3 tablespoons butter or
    shortening
2 cups diced potatoes
1 cup diced carrots
2 cups boiling water
1 teaspoon salt
¼ teaspoon paprika
2 tablespoons flour

Brown onion in 1 tablespoon fat. Add potatoes, carrots, boiling water, salt and paprika. Boil 15 minutes, covered, or until tender.
Cream flour and remaining 2 tablespoons fat together in bowl. Add to milk in double boiler. Cook and stir until smooth. Combine sauce with vegetables. Serves 4–6. Very good.

Party Sandwich Loaf

Good accompaniment to a salad lunch, e.g., 24 Hour Salad (page 100).
Purchase sliced French bread. Use when a day old.
Soften and mix:
1 pound Velveeta cheese
2 tablespoons butter
celery salt and paprika to taste

Spread slices to edges generously. Pack all in order again. Wrap in foil. Bake at
325° for 1 hour.
To prepare in advance, refrigerate 1–2 days, then bake at 350° for 1 hour.

Party Buns

1 package cream cheese *or*
1 cup shredded
   cheddar cheese
1 can tuna *or*
1 cup chicken, turkey or
   salmon
2–3 drops lemon juice
½ cup salad dressing
1–2 tablespoons chopped
   celery
1–2 tablespoons chopped
   onion
1–2 tablespoons chopped
   pepper
2 chopped hard cooked eggs

Pile into 8–10 buns (hamburger or southern
type). Wrap in foil. Bake at 400° for 15
minutes or at 325° for 30 minutes.

These may have additional variations of
chopped pickles, relish, tomatoes and olives.

Main Dishes

Sweet and Sour Chicken Wings

2 pounds chicken wings
⅔ cup brown sugar
2 tablespoons vinegar
2 tablespoons soy sauce
salt and pepper
garlic powder
cube of chicken
 bouillon

Split joints of chicken wings, flour and brown in a little fat. Lay them flat (the flatter the better) in a baking dish. For each pound of chicken, crumble across the top ⅓ cup brown sugar; over that sprinkle 2 tablespoons vinegar and 2 tablespoons soy sauce, a little garlic powder and a cube of chicken bouillon crumbled across the top. Add salt and pepper to your own taste. Put cover on dish, and bake for 45 minutes in 325° oven.

Serve with rice. In rice place sauteed mushrooms and green pepper. Also serve a tossed salad. Serves 4.

Spareribs can be substituted for chicken wings. The ribs cut into 1 inch pieces. Use same method as for wings but increase baking time to 1 hour.

Sweet and Sour Meatballs

1½ pounds ground beef
2 eggs
3 tablespoons flour
¾ cup oil
1½ cups chicken bouillon
3 large green peppers, diced
6 slices pineapple, diced
2 tablespoons cornstarch
2 tablespoons soy sauce
1 tablespoon Accent
¾ cup vinegar
¾ cup pineapple juice
¾ cup cup sugar
½ teaspoon salt
pepper

Shape ground beef into 18 balls. Combine flour and eggs, salt and pepper. Dip meatballs into mixture and brown. Keep hot. Pour out all but 1 tablespoon oil from skillet, and add ½ cup bouillon, green pepper and pineapple. Cover and cook over medium heat for 10 minutes. Mix remaining ingredients and add. Cook, stirring constantly until mixture comes to a boil and thickens. Add meatballs and simmer for 15 minutes. Serve with rice.

Note: This can be made up and reheated to serve with rice a day or so later—in fact I believe the flavor improves!

Hamburger Roll-Ups

Meat Filling
1 medium chopped onion
1 pound ground beef
1 tablespoon oil
½ teaspoon salt
pinch of pepper

Cook together slowly until meat is cooked.
Then add: 2 tablespoons flour, ½ cup milk.
Cook a few minutes until thickened. Cool.

Mix biscuit dough from 2 cups Bisquick
following directions on package.
Roll out dough about ½ inch thick. Cover with
meat filling. Roll up like cinnamon roll. Cut in
1½ inch slices. Put on ungreased pans and
bake 20–30 minutes at 375° or until done.
Serve with sauce (recipe below).

Sauce for Roll-Ups

1 can mushroom soup
½ cup milk
⅛ cup chili sauce

Simmer together several minutes and serve
over Hamburger Roll-Ups (recipe above).

Baked Ham

8 slices home-cured ham
8 tablespoons brown sugar
3 tablespoons dry mustard
2 cups milk

Bake in a covered casserole at 325° for
1½ hours.
This is a very old recipe.

The only part of the hog the packers waste is
the squeal—and the consumers furnish that!

Barbecued Spareribs

3 pounds spareribs
1 medium onion, chopped
1 tablespoon butter
1 tablespoon vinegar
1 tablespoon sugar
2 teaspoons salt
3 tablespoons lemon juice
½ tablespoon prepared
   mustard
½ cup water
½ cup chopped celery
dash of pepper
1 to 2 tablespoons
   Worcestershire sauce,
   if desired

Wipe ribs with damp cloth; cut in serving size pieces. Place in a shallow baking pan and bake uncovered in a moderate oven (350°) for 30 minutes. Meanwhile, lightly brown onion in butter, then add remaining ingredients. Mix well and simmer 5 minutes. Pour over the spareribs and continue baking for an hour longer, basting ribs from time to time with the sauce in the bottom of the pan. Serves 5.

Leftover Turkey or Chicken Croquettes

Cut up the leftover turkey or put through a coarse chopper.
Mix: 2 parts turkey and 1 part dressing.
Moisten with gravy. Form into patties and freeze.
To use: dip in flour, beaten egg and then bread crumbs.
Fry in oil. These can be a real unexpected company helper.

Beef Stroganoff

Cut 1½ pounds sliced round steak into thin strips. Dust with ¼ cup flour, dash of pepper. In large skillet, brown meat in ¼ cup margarine. Add 1 4-ounce can sliced mushrooms (drained), ½ cup chopped onion, 1 small clove garlic, and brown lightly. Stir in 1 can beef broth, cover. Cook for 1 hour or until meat is tender, stir now and then. Gradually stir in 1 cup sour cream. Cook over low heat 5 minutes. Serve over 3 cups cooked noodles. Serves 4.

Beef Oriental

Brown 1½ pounds ground
   beef—drain
To this add:
2 medium onions, chopped
1 cup diced celery
½ cup uncooked rice
1 cup water or beef stock

Simmer until rice is nearly soft.
Add:
1 can cream of chicken soup
1 can mushroom soup
pepper to taste
¼ cup soy sauce
½ cup water
1 can bean sprouts, drained

Blend all together well. Bake at 350° for ½ hour covered. Uncover and add Chinese noodles to the top of casserole. Leave in oven another 15 minutes and serve.
This is a Chinese supper dish.

Ribbon Meat Loaf

1 pound hamburger
onions and seasonings
   to taste
1 or 2 eggs

Dressing
1½ cups bread crumbs
   (I use whole wheat)
raisins and onions to taste
poultry seasoning and sage
   if desired
beef or chicken stock to
   moisten
margarine or butter

Mix ingredients for meat loaf. Spread one layer in greased loaf pan. Mix together the dressing. Put a layer on top of the meat. Alternate layers until finished. Bake 1¼ hours at 350°.
If desired top with mashed potatoes in the last half hour of cooking. Serves 6 to 8.

Juicy Meat Loaf

1 pound hamburger
1 egg
8 soda crackers (rolled fine)
salt and pepper
⅓ to ½ cup cream
1 small onion, chopped fine
a little catsup

Mix together lightly and shape into loaf. Make 2 shallow ditches lengthwise and spread with the following mixture:
¼ cup catsup
1 tablespoon vinegar
2 tablespoons brown sugar
2 teaspoons prepared mustard
1 teaspoon Worcestershire sauce

Bake slowly about 1½ hours at 300–325°.

Pickled Heart and Tongue

1 beef tongue
1 beef heart
1½ cups vinegar
½ cup water
salt and pepper
    to taste

Scald tongue and remove outer skin. Trim fat off heart. Boil meat until tender. Cool. Slice meat in thin slices. Heat vinegar and water, salt and pepper. Add meat and heat to boiling point. Put in jars and seal.

Other seasoning can be used if desired. This would be kept on hand for special occasions or as an emergency meat supply. Delicious in sandwiches.

Option: Vinegar dressing may be poured over whole tongue in a bowl. Cut thin slices as needed to serve.

Steak Rouladin

6 *thin slices*
 top round steak
2 pounds *or* 2 10-ounce cans
 mushrooms, sliced
garlic salt
salt and pepper
2 cups boiling water
2 beef bouillon cubes
2 tablespoons prepared
 mustard

Have butcher slice steak very thin. Each slice makes 2 rolls. Sprinkle each slice of meat with garlic salt, salt and pepper.

Spread mushrooms generously on meat and roll each up like a jelly roll. Secure with toothpicks or string. Brown on all sides in a frying pan containing about 2 tablespoons butter.

Remove to roast pan. Add the boiling water, beef bouillon cubes and mustard to frying pan and stir until all is blended. Pour over steak rolls.

Bake in 325° oven 2½ hours. Serves 6. Turn rolls once or twice during baking time.

Note: Onions are good and cheaper than sliced mushrooms.

2 cans of consomme can be used instead of bouillon cubes and boiling water.

Spanish Veal

4 tablespoons shortening
1 pound cubed stewing veal
4 tablespoons chopped
 onion
4 tablespoons chopped
 celery
4 tablespoons chopped
 green pepper
 (4 tablespoons = ¼ cup)
4 tablespoons flour
½ teaspoon salt
¼ teaspoon paprika
1½ cups canned tomatoes

Brown veal, onion, celery and pepper in hot fat in frying pan. Add flour and mix, then mix with rest of ingredients in casserole or small roasting pan. Cover and bake in slow oven at 300° for an hour, stirring occasionally. Serves 3. When doubling or tripling recipe extend baking time to 2 or 3 hours. Good served over rice.

Pork Chops

6 lean pork chops ¾ inch thick
1 tablespoon oil
4 cups sliced apples
¼ cup raisins
¼ teaspoon cinnamon
1 teaspoon grated lemon peel
    (optional)
¼ cup brown sugar
¼ cup water

Brown chops in oil in electric fry pan at 380°. Cover and cook at 200° until tender, about ½ hour. Pour off fat. Add apples, raisins, cinnamon, peel (if used), sugar and water. Cover and cook until apples are tender, 15–20 minutes. Serve on warmed platter. Serves 6.

Pork Chops and Rice Colonial

4 pork chops
1 cup uncooked rice
¼ cup chopped onion
½ teaspoon pepper
½ cup chopped green peppers
    or mushrooms
1 can consomme soup
1 cup water
2 teaspoons salt
soy sauce may be served at
    the table

Brown chops in fry pan. Place chops in casserole. Drain off excess fat in fry pan and lightly brown rice, onion and mushrooms. Spoon rice mixture over chops in casserole. Add consomme, water, salt and pepper. Cover and bake at 350° for 1 hour.

Tea Biscuits Supreme

2 cups flour, pastry and
    all-purpose combined
½ teaspoon salt
4 teaspoons baking powder
½ teaspoon cream of tartar
2 teaspoons sugar
½ cup shortening or lard
½–⅔ cup milk

Sift flour, salt, baking powder, cream of tartar and sugar. Cut in shortening until mixture resembles coarse crumbs. Add milk all at once and stir just until thoroughly mixed. Pat or roll ¾ inch thick and cut with biscuit cutter. Bake on ungreased cookie sheet at 450° for 10–12 minutes. Makes about 15 biscuits Serve with Stewed Chicken Dinner (recipe on page 92).

Stewed Chicken Dinner with Biscuits

1 4–5 pound chicken
  disjointed
Cover with water and add:
2 teaspoons salt
½ cup chopped celery
½ teaspoon pepper

Cook slowly until very tender. Remove meat from bones and cut into 1 inch pieces and return to broth.
Add: ½ can cream of mushroom soup
  ½ can cream of celery soup, undiluted
Thicken broth with a mixture of flour and water to desired thickness and when ready to serve add 1–1½ cups cooked peas and carrots. Serve over Tea Biscuits Supreme (recipe on page 91).
Variation: Roasted turkey can be substituted for chicken.

Bread Dressing

1 loaf bread,
  toasted and cubed
¼ pound butter
1 cup chopped celery
1 medium onion, chopped
3 large eggs
2 cups milk
1 cup water
1 tablespoon parsley
½ teaspoon sage
½ teaspoon poultry seasoning
1 teaspoon saffron
1 teaspoon salt
¼ teaspoon pepper

Cook onions and celery in butter over medium heat. Do not brown. Toast bread and cube. Beat eggs and add all seasonings, liquid, cooked celery and onion and bread. Mix together. Stuff fowl or bake in casserole about 1 hour in 350° oven.

If desired cook onion and celery. Let cool, then mix all other ingredients just before stuffing fowl.

Easy Dressing for Turkey

For 1 loaf bread boil 2 chopped onions in cup water for 5 minutes. Add ¼ pound (or less) butter. When it is melted add it to the chopped bread and other seasonings to taste. Salt, pepper, poultry seasoning and parsley.

A large turkey will take 2 loaves of bread.

Baked Liver

1–1½ pounds liver
Dip in flour to cover meat, then fry in 2 tablespoons hot oil. When browned on both sides, remove and place in an oven dish and cover with sauce which includes:
1 chopped onion
1 teaspoon dry mustard
1 teaspoon paprika
1 tablespoon butter
4 teaspoons brown sugar
dash of hot pepper sauce
⅓ cup chili sauce
2 tablespoons vinegar
Simmer sauce for 10 minutes, then pour over liver and bake at 300–350° for 1 hour.

Baked Fish en Papillote

1 pound fish fillets
⅓ cup melted butter
parsley
salt
dill weed
lemon juice
(carrots, onion rings,
    Swiss cheese, optional)

Use any kind of fish fillets your family likes. Thaw if necessary. Sprinkle each piece with salt and pepper on each side. Make a sauce of butter and other ingredients, all quantities to taste. Make squares of aluminum foil for each piece of fish. Spread with some of the butter mixture. Place a piece of fish on each and garnish with thinly sliced carrots, onion rings, a piece of Swiss cheese if desired. Divide remaining butter sauce evenly among fish pieces, pour over each fillet. Fold up foil securely to make a packet. Place on baking sheet and bake at 400° for 20–40 minutes depending on thickness of fish.

This can also be done in a flat casserole or baking dish and covered.

Chicken Pot Pie

Cut 1 chicken into pieces, a boiling fowl preferred. Add water to cover and cook until meat is done. Remove meat.

Season to taste and add water to make at least 4 cups. You may need some additional commercial chicken broth mix, salt, pepper and parsley to season it. Add about 4 quartered potatoes. Top with Dough for Pot Pie (recipe below).

Dough for Pot Pie

1½ cups flour
½ teaspoon salt
2 eggs
3 tablespoons cream

Push a well in flour and pour egg and cream in and mix. Stir into a soft dough. Roll thin and cut into 2–3 inch squares.

Drop carefully on surface of boiling broth. Each piece should remain flat. Cook 30 minutes in tightly covered pot. Serve in large tureen that has the warm chicken in bottom.

The old recipe says: "To each egg add half an eggshell full of cream and then enough flour to make a soft dough." An old family favorite.

Desserts

Cheese Cake

Mix together:
2 cups crushed graham wafers
½ cup melted butter
Pack in buttered pan, saving ¼ cup crumbs for top.

Dissolve 1 package lemon-lime gelatin in
¾ cup boiling water.
Allow to partially jell.
Beat together:
8 ounces cream cheese
1 large can evaporated milk
1 cup white sugar

Everybody's favorite!

Add to gelatin mixture and pour over crumb crust. Top with remaining crumbs.

Cut Glass Cake

1 package each lime, strawberry, cherry, lemon gelatin.
Dissolve each package in 1 cup hot water and add ½ cup cold water.
Pour gelatin mixtures into separate square pans and allow to jell overnight.

Prepare crumb crust as follows:
Mix together 1½ cups graham wafer crumbs, ¼ cup brown sugar, ¼ cup melted butter.
Pat into 9x13 inch pan, reserving ¼ cup for top.
Bake at 300° for 15 minutes, then cool.

Dissolve 1 package lemon gelatin in ½ cup hot pineapple juice. Add ¼ cup sugar and ½ cup cold water. Chill until beginning to jell.
Prepare 2 packages whipped topping mix according to directions on package.
Fold partly jelled lemon gelatin into whipped topping and refrigerate. Cut into squares the pans of set gelatin, and mix squares into whipped topping mixture.
Pour into crumb crust and top with reserved crumbs. Chill and cut into squares to serve.

Mandarin Orange Delight

Mix together:
2 cups graham wafer crumbs
¼ pound butter or margarine
Pat into pan, reserve ¾ cup for top.

Dissolve 2 packages orange gelatin in hot syrup from 1 can mandarin or tangerine oranges, plus enough hot water to measure 2 cups.
Add 2 cups cold water.
Allow to partly set.

Prepare 2 packages whipped topping mix according to directions on package.
Fold gelatin mixture into topping, adding orange sections.
Pour over crumbs in pan and top with remaining crumbs.

Chill several hours.

Bavarian Cream

In top of double boiler mix:
1 envelope unflavored gelatin
¼ cup sugar, ⅛ teaspoon salt

Beat together:
2 egg yolks, 1¼ cups milk
Add to gelatin mixture.
Place over boiling water and stir constantly until gelatin dissolves (about 5 minutes).
Add 1 teaspoon vanilla
Chill until consistency of egg whites.

Beat 2 egg whites until stiff.
Gradually add ¼ cup sugar while beating.
Fold gelatin mixture into the stiffly beaten egg whites.
Fold this mixture into 1 cup heavy cream, whipped (or use 1 package prepared whipped topping mix).

Pour into six-cup mold or into six individual molds.

Orange Delight Dessert

Prepare as directed on package:
1 angel food cake mix
Bake in 10 inch tube pan and cool.

Filling and frosting
Mix in heavy kettle and cook until thick, stirring constantly:
1 cup sugar
4 tablespoons cornstarch
1 tablespoon grated orange rind
1½ tablespoons lemon juice
½ teaspoon salt
1 cup orange juice
2 egg yolks

Remove from heat and stir in:
¼ cup butter
Cool to room temperature.

Prepare according to directions:
1 package whipped topping mix and fold into cooled filling. Cut cake in half crosswise to make 2 layers. Place 1 layer on large cake plate and cover with ¼ filling mixture. Top with second cake layer and frost sides and top with remaining filling mixture. Garnish with maraschino cherries. Cover and store in cool place for 24 hours.

7¢ Pudding

Mix 1 cup brown sugar, butter size of an egg. Add alternately 1 cup sweet milk and 2 cups flour sifted with 1 teaspoon soda, ½ teaspoon cream of tartar and ¼ teaspoon nutmeg. Add ½ cup raisins. Pour into bowl and steam 3 hours.

This would cost a little more at today's prices!

24 Hour Salad

In top of double boiler mix:
3 egg yolks
**2 tablespoons vinegar or
    lemon juice**
2 tablespoons sugar
1 tablespoon butter
few grains salt
Cook until thick, then cool.

Whip until stiff, 1 cup cream. Fold into
cooled dressing.

Add following fruits (or see variations)
1 cup drained pitted cherries
2 cups drained pineapple chunks
2 cups sliced oranges
24 cut marshmallows

Variations: bananas, mandarin oranges,
maraschino cherries

Refrigerate 24 hours.

Spoon into lettuce cups. Hot biscuits or "Party
Sandwich Loaf " (page 81) go well with it.

Apple Delight

Mix together:
1 quart sliced apples
¾ cup sugar
1 tablespoon flour
1 teaspoon cinnamon
Place in greased casserole.

Topping
Combine 1 cup oatmeal
¾ cup brown sugar
½ cup flour
¼ teaspoon soda
¼ teaspoon baking powder
**Rub in ¼ cup melted butter
    to make crumbs**

Sprinkle crumbs on top of apple mixture.

Bake at 375° for 35–40 minutes.
Delicious served hot with vanilla ice cream.

Apple Salad (a quick dessert)

Peel, core and dice 6 or 7
    large Spy apples
Add 1 sliced banana (optional)

Sauce
Mix in saucepan:
1 cup brown sugar
1 tablespoon butter or
    margarine
2 tablespoons flour

Heat, stirring constantly, until bubbly and
brown.
Add 1 teaspoon lemon juice and ½ cup cream
or evaporated milk.
Keep stirring until it thickens and is smooth.

Cool slightly and pour over apples.
Mix until apples are coated.

Apple Pudding

Cream together ½ cup butter
    and 1 cup sugar
Add 2 eggs, beaten, and 1 cup
    sour cream
Sift together and add:
2 cups sifted flour
1 teaspoon baking powder
1 teaspoon baking soda
½ teaspoon salt

Beat until batter is light and add 1 teaspoon
vanilla.
Pare and core 2 or 3 apples.
Slice and toss into mixture of ¼ cup sugar and
½ teaspoon cinnamon.
Pour more than half the batter into a warm
and greased pan (9 inch square).
Arrange apple slices evenly over batter and
top with remaining batter.
Bake at 350° for 30 minutes.
Reduce heat to 325° and continue to bake 14
minutes longer.
Sprinkle additional sugar and cinnamon over
top of cake and serve warm, with or without
milk.

Foamy Rum Sauce

Beat 1 egg white until stiff.
Gradually add ¼ cup corn syrup, beating constantly.
Beat 1 egg yolk until lemon colored.
Gradually add ¼ cup corn syrup and 2 teaspoons rum extract.
Fold egg yolk mixture into stiffly beaten egg white mixture and serve.

Dumplings—Lemon, Apple, Cherry, Maple Syrup

Dumplings are a simple quick dessert made on top of the stove. Use a pan with a tight-fitting lid and drop batter by spoonfuls on boiling syrup and cover. Boil on low heat 15 minutes.

Lemon Syrup:
2 cups water
1 cup sugar
1 tablespoon maple syrup
juice and rind 1 lemon

Apple Syrup:
2 cups water
2 cups apples
1 cup sugar
1 tablespoon butter

Cherry Syrup:
2 cups water
1 cup sugar
2 cups cherries
2 drops almond extract

Maple Syrup:
2 cups water
2 cups maple syrup

Batter: Sift 1 cup flour, 2 teaspoons baking powder, ½ teaspoon salt. Add ¾ cup milk or cream. Stir only until mixed.

Apple Dumplings

Sauce
Cook 2 cups brown sugar, 2 cups water, ¼ teaspoon cinnamon and simmer 5 minutes

Pastry
Pie pastry may also be used

Old fashioned goodness!

Sift together 2 cups flour, 2 teaspoons baking powder, 1 teaspoon salt. Add ½ cup shortening and blend as for pastry, and then ½ cup milk. Pat into a ball and then roll out and cut into squares large enough to cover a half or whole cored apple. Bring corners of dough to center top and pinch together. Pinch all sides together.

Pour sauce into baking dish. Place apple dumplings on top. Bake at 425° 10 minutes and then at 375° until apples are soft, about 30 minutes.

Caramel Pudding

Heat 2 tablespoons butter and
1 cup brown sugar until golden brown.
Add 4 cups cold milk.
Continue to heat on medium heat.
Just before boiling, add a paste mixture of:
3 tablespoons cornstarch, mixed with
⅓ cup milk.

Stir constantly until it boils. Turn off heat and cover for 3 minutes to cook starch completely.
Add 1 teaspoon vanilla.
Cool.

Prune Pudding

½ pound prunes
2 cups boiling water
Cover and boil 5 minutes.

Cool and remove stones, then add
¾ cup sugar
1 stick cinnamon (optional)
1¼ cups boiling water
Bring to boil and simmer 5 minutes.
Mix ¼ cup cornstarch with ½ cup water. Add to prune mixture and simmer 5 minutes.
Serve cold with whipped cream.

Frozen Berry Fluff

Beat 2 egg whites and 1 tablespoon lemon juice slightly in large bowl.
Gradually add 1½ cups sugar and 2 cups sliced fresh strawberries.

Beat at high speed 12–15 minutes until mixture is fluffy and has large volume.

Fold in 1 cup whipped cream or whipped topping and freeze.

Lemon Fluff Dessert

Combine:
**12 double graham wafers,
    crushed
⅛ cup melted butter
½ cup white sugar**

Pack half this mixture into a
9x13 inch pan.

Mix together:
**1 package lemon gelatin
juice and rind of 1 lemon
½ cup white sugar
1½ cups boiling water**
Chill until partly set.

Whip until very stiff:
1 large can chilled evaporated milk.
Beat gelatin mixture slightly and fold into
whipped milk.

Pour into pan and top with remaining crumbs.
Chill 24 hours.

Rhubarb Tarte

**1 cup flour
½ cup butter or margarine
pinch of salt
1 tablespoon sugar**
Crumb and press in pan and
bake at 350° for 10 minutes.

Filling
**3 egg yolks
1¼ cups sugar
2 tablespoons flour
rind of 1 orange
½ cup milk or cream
3 cups rhubarb, cut in pieces**

Mix filling and pour over base. Bake 1 hour.
When baked top with 3 egg whites beaten with
6 tablespoons sugar. Spread on tarte and bake
another 15 minutes.

Rhubarb Cake Pudding

Melt ⅓ cup butter in 9 inch
 square cake pan
Sprinkle melted butter with 1
 cup brown sugar and 4 cups
 cut up rhubarb
Sift together:
1⅓ cups sifted all-purpose flour
1 cup sugar
2 teaspoons baking powder
½ teaspoon salt
Add:
⅓ cup soft shortening
⅔ cup milk
1 teaspoon vanilla

Heat oven to 350°.
Beat 2 minutes medium speed on mixer.
Add 1 egg and beat 2 minutes. Pour batter
over fruit.
Bake about 40 minutes at 350°.
Serve warm with milk.
A delicious springtime dessert.

Raspberry Dessert

Dissolve 1 package raspberry gelatin in 1 cup boiling water.
Add:
1 package (10 ounces) frozen or partly thawed raspberries
1 cup sweetened applesauce

Mix together and pour into serving dish.

Top with mixture of
1 cup sour cream
1 cup miniature marshmallows

Chill until set.

*The real proof of a woman's courtesy is for one
to have an ailment just like the other woman is
describing and not tell her about it.*

Rice Fluff

Dissolve 1 3-ounce package orange or lemon gelatin in:
1 cup boiling water
Add ½ cup pineapple juice
½ cup white sugar.

When beginning to jell, whip until fluffy and add:
1 cup drained pineapple
1½ cups cooked rice
Fold in
1 cup whipped cream.
Chill.

Apple Bars

½ cup shortening
1 cup sugar
2 eggs, beaten
1 cup sifted flour
1 teaspoon baking powder
½ teaspoon soda
½ teaspoon salt
1 tablespoon cocoa
1 teaspoon cinnamon
½ teaspoon nutmeg
¼ teaspoon cloves
1 cup rolled oats
1½ cups diced peeled apples
    (Ontario apples)
½ cup walnuts,
    coarsely chopped
powdered sugar

Cream shortening and sugar until light. Beat in eggs one at a time. Sift dry ingredients except powdered sugar. Fold in rest of ingredients. Bake at 375° about 25 minutes. Cool slightly and sprinkle with powdered sugar (sifted). Makes 36 2½x1¼ inch bars. May be served as a pudding with sauce.

Spicy Fudge Pudding

Sift together into mixing bowl:
1 cup sifted all-purpose flour
2 teaspoons baking powder
¾ cup granulated sugar
⅛ teaspoon salt
2 tablespoons cocoa
¾ teaspoon cinnamon
¼ teaspoon cloves

Combine:
½ cup milk
½ teaspoon vanilla
**2 tablespoons melted butter or
  margarine**

Add to dry ingredients and stir just until
smooth. Spread over bottom of 8 inch square
buttered pan. Combine and sprinkle over
batter
½ cup firmly packed brown sugar
½ cup white sugar
Pour 1 cup cold water over entire mixture.
Do not stir.
Bake 325° 40 minutes or until top is firm to a
light touch.

Apple Butter Pudding

Beat well in order given:
2 eggs
1 cup brown sugar
3 tablespoons apple butter
1 cup sour cream

Add the sifted dry ingredients:
2 cups pastry flour
1 teaspoon soda
½ teaspoon cloves
¼ teaspoon nutmeg
1 teaspoon cinnamon
**Add ¾ cup lightly floured
  raisins**

Pour into greased casserole, cover with wax
paper and steam 1½ hours.
Serve with milk (sweetened).

Just try it once!

Dump Cake

1 19-ounce can crushed
   pineapple
1 19-ounce can strawberry or
   cherry pie filling
1 yellow cake mix
butter

Pour pineapple (including juice) into a
greased 9x13 inch pan. Pour cherries or
strawberries on top. Sprinkle with dry cake
mix and dot with butter. Bake at 350° for
one hour.

Steamed Carrot Pudding

Blend together:
1 cup sugar
½ cup lard or suet
Add:
1 cup grated carrots
1 cup grated potatoes
1 cup raisins
Sift together and add:
1½ cups flour
1 teaspoon soda
½ teaspoon cloves
½ teaspoon cinnamon
½ teaspoon nutmeg

Optional—add peel, cherries and nuts to taste.
Steam 1½ hours. Serve hot with a sauce or
milk.

Sauce
Caramelize on low heat 1 cup brown sugar,
3 tablespoons butter until rich golden
brown. Add 2 cups warm water. Stir until
dissolved. Dissolve 3 tablespoons cornstarch
in ⅓ cup water.
Add slowly to syrup mix.
Cook until it thickens.
Add 1 tablespoon vanilla.
Serve warm over pudding.

Make this for Christmas!

Home-Made Ice Cream

6 eggs, separated
2½ cups whipping cream
1 cup sugar
flavoring

Beat cream until stiff and add ⅓ cup sugar. Beat egg yolks, rest of sugar and flavoring until stiff and lemon colored. Gently fold together and add stiffly beaten egg whites last. Freeze stirring gently 3 times, once every hour to keep liquid from forming at the bottom. Yield: ½ gallon

Variations: Add 1 cup of blueberries or any fresh fruit (mashed if necessary) at third stirring.

Home-Made Ice Cream *(To be made in hand freezer.)*

Mix together and stir well
3 quarts homogenized milk
1 pint whipping cream
4 eggs, beaten
3 cups sugar
3 tablespoons vanilla
¼ teaspoon salt

Pour into hand freezer and turn about 20 minutes.

Mmm-good!

Pies and Tarts

Pastries *(Each uses pastry flour.)*

No. 1
Sift into a bowl 5 cups flour, 3 tablespoons brown sugar, 1 teaspoon baking
powder, 1 teaspoon salt.
Work into it 1 pound lard.
Into a cup break 1 egg, add 2 tablespoons vinegar.
Stir only to blend and then fill cup to ⅞ line with water. Mix well with flour. Store
in refrigerator in a tight plastic dish.
Yield: 8 single crusts

No. 2
Cut 1 pound lard into a narrow bowl.
Add 1 cup boiling water. Stir well.
Sift 6 cups pastry flour, 2 teaspoons sugar, 2 teaspoons baking powder, 2
teaspoons salt into a large bowl and pour the smooth lard mix into it. Stir with a
wooden spoon. Store in refrigerator bowl or heavy plastic. It freezes too.
Yield: 9 single crusts

Crumbs for fruit pies
Using fingertips work thoroughly ¼ cup butter into ½ cup brown sugar, 1 cup
flour, ½ teaspoon soda.
This amount covers the thickened fruit of 3 pies, serving as a cover.

No. 3
2½ cups pastry flour, 1 teaspoon salt, ½ teaspoon baking powder sifted together.
Put ¾ cup corn oil in a cup. Add 1 tablespoon vinegar and fill with ice water.
Blend all with a fork.
Roll on wax paper.
Yield: 3 crusts

No. 4 *Quantity Recipe*
Blend with cutter or hands
14 cups flour, 1 pound lard, 1 pound shortening, 2 teaspoons salt.
Store in airtight container.
For 1 pie shell use 1¼ cups mix and sprinkle 3 tablespoons water on it. Mix until
it stays in ball. Roll.

Note about top pastry: If the top is cut smaller than the plate, leaving about 1
inch fruit showing, the steam can escape and the pie will not boil out into the
oven. Brush cover with milk and sprinkle sugar over.

Fruit Pies

Bake at 425° — 10 minutes
375° — 30 minutes

Cherry
2¾ cups cherries and juice (fresh or frozen and thawed and no sugar)
1 cup sugar
3 tablespoons quick-cooking tapioca
3 drops almond flavoring
few drops red coloring
Best results are if tapioca stands on cherries before putting into pie.
Cover with top pastry or strips.

Peach
Make same as cherry pie.

Blueberry or Elderberry
Same as cherry except ⅓ cup finely cut rhubarb or 3 tablespoons lemon juice
will give the needed tartness.

Elderberry
Spread 1 cup applesauce over the bottom of the unbaked pie shell, and then add
1½ cups elderberries and 1 cup sugar.

Strawberry Pie

Sort 1 quart strawberries into 2 equal parts. Use the less perfect ones to crush.
Add to them ½ cup water mixed with 3 tablespoons cornstarch. Cook until thick
and clear. Add 1 cup sugar, 1 tablespoon butter, 1 tablespoon lemon juice, few
grains salt. Cool. Add remaining cut berries. Pour into baked shell. Chill. Serve
with whipped cream.

Relief Sale Strawberry Pie

This is absolutely the best way to prepare fresh strawberries! A single yet elegant recipe that brings out the natural flavor. Always a favorite at the sales during strawberry season.

Fresh frozen and thawed berries are thickened without cooking by using Sure-Jell that is mixed with sugar thoroughly and then stirred into about 2 cups berries. The baked pie shell is spread with this glaze, then fresh strawberries are pushed into it and covered with the remaining glaze. Top with whipped cream or a good substitute.

Rhubarb Pie with Meringue

Fill a 10 inch pastry shell with 3 cups finely cut strawberry rhubarb.
Mix 1½ cups sugar, 3 tablespoons flour, 1 tablespoon lemon or orange rind and juice, ¼ teaspoon salt, and 2 egg yolks.
Pour this over the rhubarb and bake at 425° 10 minutes and then 375° 30 minutes.
When the pie is nearly baked beat the egg whites stiff, add 3 tablespoons sugar, ½ teaspoon cornstarch and ¼ teaspoon baking powder.
Pour over pie that is baked and brown in the oven until golden peaks appear. The above meringue rises like a cloud and cuts like a charm. Can be used on any pie.

Luscious Apple Pie

Make a syrup of 1 cup sugar, ½ cup water.
Add 6–8 apples that have been sliced.
Simmer 5 minutes. Add 2 tablespoons butter and 1 teaspoon almond extract.
Stir well and cook longer if apples are not done. Cool and place in a baked shell.
Make crumbs to put on top:
¾ cup flour, ½ cup brown sugar, ⅓ cup butter. Bake at 425° just until crumbs are brown.

Dutch Apple Pie

Crumbs
1 cup brown sugar
⅓ cup flour
½ teaspoon cinnamon
Spread ⅓ of these on bottom
of pastry.

Cover this with small wedges of apples, about 7. The top layer may be arranged in fancy design; e.g. sixths in a circle. Cover apples with remaining crumbs. Spoon over them one of the following:
½ cup sour cream
¼ cup milk
¼ cup water and 2 tablespoons lemon juice.
If milk or water are used, dot with butter for additional glaze.
Bake at 450° 10 minutes, then at 375° for 40 minutes.

Maple Walnut or Pecan Pie

Beat 3 eggs and add ¾ cup brown sugar, 2 tablespoons flour, 1¼ cups maple syrup (mix with corn syrup if you wish), ¼ cup melted butter.
Chop in 1 cup coarsely cut walnuts or pecans.
Pour into an unbaked 10 inch pie shell.
Sprinkle nuts on top.
Bake at 400° 10 minutes and 375° 30 minutes.

Grape Pie

Wash and then squeeze the pulp from the skins. Cook pulp 5 minutes and press through a sieve to separate the seeds.
Beat 1 egg, add 1 cup sugar, 2 tablespoons flour, 1 tablespoon butter, 1 tablespoon lemon juice. Add the skins and the pulp.

Pour into unbaked pie shell and covered with a lattice top of pastry strips or top with crumbs. May bake uncovered and serve with whites of egg beaten and 2 tablespoons sugar.

Crumbs: ¼ cup flour, ¼ cup sugar, 2 tablespoons butter

Winter Peach Pie

Fill unbaked pie shell with well drained canned peaches.
Cream together ⅔ cup (scant) sugar, 2 tablespoons butter, 1 heaping
tablespoon flour, 2 tablespoons lemon juice.
Add 1 egg, ¼ teaspoon cinnamon or nutmeg, ⅓ cup peach juice.
Pour over peaches and bake 10 minutes at 400°, reducing heat to 350°
until baked.

Lemon Sponge Pie

Beat in the order given:
2 egg yolks
grated rind and juice of
    1 lemon
1 cup sugar
3 tablespoons flour
3 tablespoons butter
¼ teaspoon salt
1 cup milk
Add 2 beaten egg whites

Pour into unbaked pie shell.
Preheat oven to 425°, put in the pies and
reduce to 350° for 40 minutes.

Shoofly Pie

For 1 deep 10 inch pie. Mix 1 cup maple syrup (or you may dilute it with corn
syrup if you wish), ¾ cup cold water and ¾ teaspoon soda which has been
dissolved in ¼ cup hot water.
Make crumb mixture: 1 cup pastry flour, ⅔ cup brown sugar, ¼ teaspoon salt,
2 tablespoons butter. Work the butter into the flour and sugar with fingertips.
Remove about ⅔ cup crumbs and mix the rest with the liquid. Pour it into the
pie shell. Sprinkle the ⅔ cup crumbs over top. Bake at 425° 20 minutes and at
325° 20 minutes.

Vanilla Pie

A Sale Pie

Mix 2 cups brown sugar and 5 tablespoons flour. Add to it 1 cup maple syrup, and 4 cups hot water. Cook until starch is cooked and it is syrupy. Cool and add 2 teaspoons vanilla.

Make crumb mixture: Using fingertips blend 2 cups flour, 1 cup brown sugar, 1 teaspoon soda, 1 teaspoon cream of tartar and 1 cup butter. Divide the juice into 3 unbaked pie shells and then divide the crumbs over the 3 pies.

Bake 425° 10 minutes and reduce to 325° 25 minutes.

Easy Pumpkin Pie

1 cup sugar
1 or 2 eggs
1 cup pumpkin
1 tablespoon flour

Beat all with beater and add 1 cup milk. Moisten the unbaked pie shell with egg white before adding to it the filling. Sprinkle the moist shell with nutmeg. Sprinkle a generous coating of cinnamon over top of pie. Bake 425° 10 minutes and reduce to 325° 25 minutes.

Sour Cream Elderberry Pie

Combine 1 cup sugar, 2 tablespoons flour, 1 cup sour cream and 2 cups elderberries.Pour into 9 inch pie shell and bake 425° 15 minutes and then at 375°–350° for 30 minutes.

Regular cow cream preferred. Dairy sour cream can be used for part.

Rhubarb-Strawberry Pie

Stir ¼ cup flour into 1½ cups diced rhubarb.

Add 1¼ cups strawberries and juice, 1 cup sugar, 2 tablespoons quick-cooking tapioca, 2 drops red coloring.

Dorda Pie

Pastry
8 cups pastry flour
2⅔ teaspoons salt
2⅔ cups lard *or* 2 cups lard
    with ⅔ cup shortening or
    butter

Sift flour and salt together. Cut in lard as you would in regular pastry.

1 egg
¾ cup commercial sour cream
1¼ teaspoons cream of tartar
2½ teaspoons baking powder
½ cup sugar

Whip the five ingredients together and add to the flour mixture.

Filling
8 cups of unsweetened
    applesauce. (Cook apples
    with as little water as
    possible.)
⅛ teaspoon salt
2½ cups white sugar
1 teaspoon cinnamon
2 pounds raisins, washed

Line 5 pie plates with pastry a little thicker than usual. Add applesauce mixture. Cut strips for lattice top at least ³⁄₁₆ inch thick. Arrange on pie, and with a pastry brush spread the strips with a mixture of an egg yolk and milk. Bake at 450° 20 minutes and 350° 30–40 minutes. Use strips of aluminum foil around the edge of pie plate to prevent pastry from getting too dark.

Gooseberry Pie Filling

2⅔ cups gooseberries, ½ cup of it may be water
1⅓ cups sugar, 3 tablespoons quick-cooking tapioca
2 tablespoons lemon juice

Raisin Cream Pie

Mix and cook in double boiler 2 eggs, ¾ cup sugar, 3 tablespoons flour, 2 cups milk, ¾ cup raisins that have been puffed by standing in boiling water. Add vanilla and raisins last. Pour into baked crust. Serve with whipped cream.

Montgomery County or Lemon Drop Pie

Part 1
In double boiler cook:
Juice and rind of 2 lemons, 2 cups sugar, 2 tablespoons flour, 3 beaten eggs,
4 cups milk
This is a thin sauce.

Part 2 is like a soft cookie dough.
Cream ½ cup butter, 1 cup sugar. Add ½ cup sweet milk and 1 teaspoon soda that
is sifted into 1¼ cups flour.

Divide Part 1 evenly into three 9 inch pie plates and drop spoonfuls of Part 2
evenly on each plate. Do not stir. Bake at 425° 10 minutes and at 350° 30
minutes.
It is better second or third day! Lemon flavor saturates the top layer more.

These are "Old Timers"

Apple Butter Pie

Beat ½ cup apple butter, 2 eggs, ½ cup brown sugar, 1½ teaspoons cornstarch,
1 teaspoon cinnamon. Add 2 cups milk and beat slowly.
Pour into unbaked 10 inch pie shell. It may be covered with strips of pastry laid
in lattice fashion. Bake at 425° 10 minutes, 350° 30 minutes.

Grasshopper Pie

24 cream-filled chocolate
   cookies—crushed
¼ cup margarine, melted
¼ cup milk
few drops peppermint extract
few drops green food coloring
1 jar marshmallow creme
2 cups heavy cream, whipped

Combine cookie crumbs and margarine. Press
into 9 inch spring pan, reserving ½ cup of
mixture for topping. Gradually add milk,
extract and food coloring to marshmallow
creme, mixing until well blended. Fold in
whipped cream. Pour into pan, sprinkle with
remaining crumbs. Freeze. Remove half hour
before serving.

You'll like this kind of grasshopper in your house!

Green Tomato Mincemeat

This can be made after the first frost.

Mix together:
6 cups chopped apples
6 cups chopped green
   tomatoes
4 cups brown sugar
1½ cups vinegar
3 cups raisins
2 cups currants
1 teaspoon cloves
1 teaspoon allspice
1 teaspoon mace
1 teaspoon pepper
1 tablespoon cinnamon
2 teaspoons salt

Simmer for 3 hours.
Add ¾ cup butter.
Pour into clean hot jars and seal.

Mincemeat

1½ pounds beef
1½ pounds pork
½ pound suet
2 pounds seedless raisins
2 pounds currants
2 pounds granulated sugar
1 pound brown sugar
2 oranges
2 lemons
½ pound citron peel
2 quarts peeled and
   cored apples
1 cup molasses
2 teaspoons ground cloves
3 teaspoons cinnamon
3 teaspoons nutmeg
1 cup cider

Cook beef, pork and suet until tender. Mince fine or put through chopper. Put the apples, oranges and lemons through chopper. Mix all ingredients thoroughly. Bring to a boil and simmer 12 minutes. Put in jars and seal while hot.

You can freeze it too!

Pineapple Bavarian Pie

Make a graham cracker crust:
1½ cups crumbs, ¼ cup butter, ¼ cup brown sugar.
Press into 9 inch plate and bake 10 minutes at 350°.

Filling

Bring to a boil 1¼ cups crushed pineapple,
add 1 package lemon gelatin
½ cup sugar
½ teaspoon lemon rind
2 teaspoons lemon juice
Stir until all is dissolved. Cool until it thickens slightly.
Have ready 1 cup chilled evaporated milk to which add 1 tablespoon lemon juice. Beat until stiff. Fold it into the chilled pineapple mixture. Chill slightly.
Pour into graham cracker shell and chill until time to serve.

Coconut Pie

Mix in top of double boiler:
1 envelope unflavored gelatin
¼ cup sugar
⅛ teaspoon salt
Beat together 3 eggs yolks and 1¾ cups milk. Add to gelatin mixture.
Cook, stirring constantly until gelatin dissolves.
Remove from heat and stir in 1 teaspoon vanilla.
Chill, stirring occasionally until mixture mounds.
Stir in ¾ cup flaked coconut.

Make meringue of 3 egg whites and ¼ cup sugar. Fold into gelatin mixture and pile in baked 9 inch pie shell. Chill.

Top can be garnished with maraschino cherries, or fresh fruits in season.
A delicious company pie that can be prepared a day ahead of time.

Buttermilk Pie

Combine 1 cup sugar, 2 tablespoons flour, ½ teaspoon soda. Beat 2 tablespoons melted butter, 2 eggs, 1 teaspoon lemon juice.
Add the sugar mixture and 2 cups buttermilk.
Pour into unbaked 10 inch pie shell.
Bake at 425° 10 minutes and at 350° 35 minutes.

Butter Tarts

Pastry
2 cups shortening
7 cups pastry flour
¾ cup skim milk powder
1½ teaspoons salt
⅞ cup brown sugar
2 large eggs
⅞ cup water
1 teaspoon vanilla
6–8 drops yellow food
   coloring (optional)

Blend all dry ingredients except brown sugar with shortening. Beat eggs, brown sugar, water, coloring and vanilla together. Mix with dry ingredients as any dough mixture.
Yield: 4½ dozen shells

Filling 1
5 cups brown sugar
5 eggs
1 cup butter
½ cup milk

Mix well in mixer. Fill tart shell ⅔ with filling. Makes 4½ dozen.

Filling 2
2 eggs
1 cup brown sugar
1 cup maple syrup
4 tablespoons butter
1 teaspoon vanilla

Beat until thickness of cream.

Note: Coconut, nuts or raisins may be added as desired.

Pickles and
Relishes

Mother's Favorite Pickle

1 quart raw cabbage,
  chopped fine
1 quart dark red beets
  (boiled and skinned),
  chopped fine
2 cups white sugar
  (more if desired)
1 tablespoon salt
1 teaspoon pepper
1 cup horseradish
1 teaspoon mustard
1 teaspoon ginger (optional)

Cover all ingredients with vinegar which has been diluted with the juice in which beets were boiled. Heat just to boiling point. (Do not allow to boil, as boiling fades color of beets.) Although recipe calls for equal quantities of cabbage and beets, this relish looks much nicer if more beets than cabbage are used.

Fruit and Tomato Relish
Sometimes called End of Season Relish.

6-quart basket peeled
  tomatoes
6 large pears
6 large apples
6 large peaches
4 onions

Chop fruits and vegetables finely.
Add 4 cups granulated sugar, 2 tablespoons salt, ½ cup pickling spices (tied loosely in bag), 1 pint vinegar.
Simmer in large kettle for 1 hour, stirring often. Remove spice bag and seal in hot sterile jars.
Note: Chopped red and green sweet pepper may also be added.

Tomato Butter

Peel and cut in small pieces 12 medium tomatoes. Add 1½ cups white sugar and boil 1 hour, stirring often to prevent sticking. Add 2 cups white vinegar, 1 teaspoon salt, 1 teaspoon whole cinnamon, 1 teaspoon cloves (tied in bag). Boil until thick.

To clean brass rub catsup on a soft cloth and polish. Rinse.

Pickled Watermelon Rind

To prepare rind, trim off outer green skin and most of pink flesh, leaving only a bit of pink on white rind.
Cut rind into 1½x1¾ inch pieces.
Soak 9 cups prepared rind overnight in brine of 3 tablespoons salt and 4 cups water.
In morning drain, cover with fresh water and cook until tender.
Heat to boiling point, 4 cups white sugar, 2 cups white vinegar, 2 cups water.
Add 6 cinnamon sticks, 2 tablespoons whole cloves, 2 tablespoons whole allspice (tied in cloth bag).
Add cooked rind and simmer until rind is transparent—about 45 minutes.
Pack hot rind in sterile jars.
Remove spice bag from syrup and bring again to boil.
Pour boiling syrup over rind, making sure syrup completely covers rind.
Seal jars.

Pickled Eggs

2 cups vinegar
1 cup water
½ cup white sugar
salt and pepper
2 bay leaves

Boil until sugar is dissolved.
Cool and add cold peeled hard-boiled eggs.
Best after standing about 2 days.

Copper Pickles

Slice in thin slices about 1 gallon (30) cucumbers and 6–8 onions in thin rings.
Add ½ cup pickling salt to ice water and cover the cucumber and onion slices.
Let stand at least 3 hours or overnight. Drain well.
Boil 2 cups vinegar, 2 cups sugar, 2 teaspoons mustard seed, 2 teaspoons celery seed, 1 teaspoon turmeric, 1 teaspoon whole cloves. Mix well and bring to boil.
Add slices and bring again to boiling point. Seal in sterile jars.

Company Best Pickles

Scrub and cover with boiling water 10 medium sized cucumbers.
Let stand 24 hours and drain.
Repeat 3 times (4 days in all).
One 5th day drain and cut into serving pieces.
Combine:
8 cups white sugar
4 cups vinegar
2 tablespoons pickling spices
5 teaspoons salt
2 cups water
few drops green food coloring
Bring above mixture to boil and pour over drained and sliced cucumbers.
Let stand 48 hours, then bring to a boil and seal in sterile jars.

Cucumber Relish

12 cups cucumbers, chopped fine
1 quart onions, chopped fine
1 large head cauliflower, chopped
4 red sweet peppers, chopped
Add ¼ cup salt and let stand overnight.

Next morning, drain well and add:
8 cups white sugar
3 cups cider vinegar
1½ tablespoons mustard
2 tablespoons turmeric
1½ tablespoons celery seed
Bring to boil and add ⅔ cup flour mixed with 1 cup water.
Boil ½ hour and seal in sterile jars.

To clean your barbecue or oven racks place
them on the grass overnight or on a rainy day.
The cleanup job is easier!

Queen of Pickles

1 quart small pickling onions, peeled
1 quart small cucumbers, cut into ½ inch long pieces
3 sweet red peppers, chopped
3 sweet green peppers, chopped
At night, cover above with brine made of ½ cup coarse salt and enough boiling water to cover.
1 large head cauliflower broken into florets
Cover cauliflower with boiling water and let stand overnight.
Next morning: cook cauliflower and 1 quart very small carrots until nearly tender, and drain.
Drain brine from first mixture and rinse well.

Mix together and add:
1 quart chopped onions
1 quart chopped cucumbers
1 quart vinegar
7 cups white sugar
1 tablespoon mustard seed
1 tablespoon celery seed
Boil 5 minutes.
Make paste of ⅔ cup all-purpose flour, ¼ cup dry mustard, 2 tablespoons turmeric, ¼ cup vinegar. Add to hot pickle mixture.
Boil thoroughly to cook flour.
Seal in hot sterile jars.

Sweet Pickle Sticks

Syrup
4 cups vinegar
5 cups sugar
1 tablespoon salt
1 teaspoon ground cloves
2 tablespoons mixed pickling
   spice (tied in cloth bag)
1 teaspoon ground cinnamon

12–15 large cucumbers. Peel and remove center seeds. Cut in sticks 3–4 inches long. Cover with boiling water. Let cool and drain.

Boil syrup for 5 minutes. Add cucumber sticks and cook 5 minutes longer. Seal in sterile jars.

Mustard Bean Pickles

Cook 1 peck beans (cut in pieces) for ½ hour in weak salt water liquid and drain.
Bring to a boil 3 parts vinegar, 4 cups brown sugar.
Make a paste of:
½ cup dry mustard
½ cup flour
3 tablespoons turmeric
1 teaspoon celery seed
½ cup water
Add to vinegar and water and cook until thickened.
Add beans and cook 5 minutes longer.
Seal in sterile jars.

Pickled Beets

Syrup
4 cups vinegar
1 cup water
3 cups white sugar
½ teaspoon pepper
1½ teaspoons salt
½ teaspoon cloves
   (or pickling spice)

Boil until tender, then peel 6-quart basket beets. If beets are large, cut into pieces, and fill sterile jars.

Bring syrup ingredients to boil.

Fill jars and seal.
These beets will keep in refrigerator for some time.

Gooseberry Catsup

4 pounds gooseberries
2 pounds white sugar
½ pint vinegar
1 tablespoon cinnamon
1 tablespoon cloves
1 teaspoon black pepper
1 teaspoon salt

Boil all ingredients together about 30 minutes or until thick.
Stir frequently to prevent sticking.

Green Hot Dog Relish

4 quarts cucumbers
1 quart onions
2 bunches celery
4 red sweet peppers
4 green sweet peppers

Put ingredients through meat chopper.
Add ¼ cup salt and let stand in crock overnight.
Add 5 cups white sugar and 1 quart vinegar.
Boil slowly 1 hour.
When cold add 5 drops oil of cinnamon, 5 drop oil of cloves (or 1 teaspoon ground cinnamon, ½ teaspoon ground cloves).
Let stand 2 days at room temperature, stirring occasionally. Heat to boiling point and put in sterile jars.

Spiced Crab Apples

Boil together:
2 cups vinegar
2 cups water
2 cups sugar
Add:
1 tablespoon whole cloves
3 cinnamon sticks
1 teaspoon whole ginger
    (tied in cheesecloth bag)

Add 4 pounds washed crab apples, blossom ends removed.
Simmer until tender.
Seal in sterile jars.

Pickled Baby Corn

6 quarts husked small corn cobs
Corn must be picked just as the tassels are starting to form and the small cobs are no more than 2 inches long. Field corn is usually used. Husk and remove the small silks from cobs. Boil cobs 7 minutes in salt water.

Syrup
5 cups vinegar
4 cups white sugar
2 tablespoons pickling spices (tied in cloth bag)
Boil syrup for 5 minutes, and remove spice bag.
Pack hot corn cobs in sterile jars. Cover with boiling syrup and seal immediately.

Dill Pickles

Prick large cucumbers in several places and fill quart jars.
To each quart add: 2 tablespoons salt, ½ cup vinegar, 1 clove garlic, 2 sprigs dill (1 in center, one on top).
Fill jars with cold water. Seal and shake.
Note: This recipe does not require cooking.

Heavenly Jam

7 cups chopped rhubarb, 6 cups sugar, 20-ounce can pineapple. Boil for 20 minutes. Add 3 ounces cherry and 3 ounces pineapple gelatin powders. Stir until dissolved and put into jars. Store in refrigerator.

Tomato Marmalade *Delicious on breakfast toast.*

4 cups tomatoes peeled and cut fine, 4 cups brown sugar, 1 orange and 1 lemon shredded very fine. Mix all and cook until thick, about 20 minutes. Stir frequently.

Strawberry Rhubarb Jam

5 cups rhubarb
4 cups sugar
Mix and let stand overnight.

In morning boil 5 minutes. Add 6 ounce package strawberry gelatin. Seal into sterile jars. Store in refrigerator or cool place.

Peach Conserve

3 pounds (6 cups) ground or chopped peaches, 6 cups white sugar, ½ dozen small oranges (grind), ⅔ cup brown sugar, ⅔ cup corn syrup.
Boil all ingredients together until thick, about 20 minutes. Seal in sterile jars.

Black Currant Preserves

2 cups black currants, 2 cups cold water.
Boil 10 minutes and then mash thoroughly.
Add 2 more cups water and 6 cups sugar.
Boil 20 minutes. Seal in sterile jars. This makes a soft jam. Good on ice cream.
Our grandmothers served cream on it.

Black Currant *(a firmer jam)*

5 cups currants, 5 cups cold water. Boil 5 minutes. Mash thoroughly. Add 5 cups sugar and boil 4 minutes. Seal in sterile jars.

Punches and Drinks

Black Currant Drink

To each quart jar add ¾ cup currants and ½ cup sugar, then fill with cold water. Steam for 10 minutes. (Count time when water in steamer is rolling.) These should stand for 1 month before using.

Black Currant Lemonade

Cover about 4 quarts currants with 1 cup water and boil until fruit is soft. Strain. Reheat juice and add 1 cup sugar. Seal.
To serve use equal parts of the syrup and water with ½ lemon to each serving.

Hint about using black currants:

Boil water and currants without sugar until they are soft. Sugar added too soon makes them tough, and flavor is not released.

Grape Juice

No. 1
Put washed and stemmed grapes in a large kettle. Add water until just below the level of the grapes. Boil 5 minutes. Strain.
To each 4 cups juice add 1 cup sugar. Bring to boiling point again and seal.

No. 2
Put 1 cup washed and stemmed grapes into a sterile 1-quart sealer, add ¾ cup sugar and slowly fill with boiling water. Seal and store. In a month you can pour off a lovely juice to serve as it is or mix it with lemon and ginger ale to taste.

Note: Jars crack easily if water is poured too fast.

Tomato Juice

One 11 quart basket tomatoes. Cut coarsely.
1 stalk celery and 3 onions
Boil all together for ½ hour and then strain.
Bring juice to a boil and add:
½ cup sugar
2 tablespoons salt
2 tablespoons vinegar
Boil 5 minutes and seal.

Eggnog

4 eggs
4 cups cold milk
⅓ cup sugar
⅛ teaspoon nutmeg
⅛ teaspoon salt
½ teaspoon vanilla

Beat all together until frothy.

Raspberry Vinegar

Put about 4 quarts raspberries into a crock and cover with vinegar. Let stand in a cool place for 24 hours. Heat to boiling point and then strain. To each cup of juice add 1 cup sugar. Boil 15 minutes and seal in sterile jars.

Mint Tea

Steep 1 tea bag and 6 stems of mint with a dash of cayenne pepper in 2 cups boiling water. (Crush the mint a bit.) Strain. Add 1 cup sugar and ½ cup lemon juice. Refrigerate.
Dilute with equal parts of water when you use it.

Quantity Fruit Punch

No. 1
3 quarts pineapple juice
1½ cups lemon juice
3 cups orange juice
⅓ cup lime juice
2½ cups sugar
1 cup lightly packed
  fresh mint leaves
2 large bottles ginger ale
1 large bottle
  carbonated water
1 pint fresh strawberries,
  quartered

Combine juice, sugar, and mint; chill.

Just before serving, add remaining ingredients; pour over cake of ice in punch bowl.

Makes 75 four-ounce servings.

No. 2
2 46-ounce cans
  pineapple juice
3 6-ounce cans frozen
  orange juice
2 6-ounce cans frozen
  lemonade

Mix all the ingredients and at the very last add 12 ounces frozen strawberries, a tray of ice cubes and 8 orange slices.

Serves 25.

For the Punch Bowl

No. 3
1½ quarts pineapple juice
1 6-ounce frozen lemonade
1 12-ounce frozen orange
  juice
1 quart cranberry juice
1½ quarts cold water
1 cup sugar
½ of a 3 ounce package
  cherry gelatin dissolved in
  1 cup boiling water

Add additional red coloring if desired. Mix all together and then at serving time add 1 quart ginger ale or lemon-lime soda.

Have you ever tried adding orange or lemon sherbet to any fruit-ginger ale punch? It is good, even if it stands awhile.

Serves 35.

Fruit Punch for 50

Boil and then cool 3 cups sugar and 3 cups water. Steep for 7 minutes ¼ cup tea or mint and 3 cups boiling water, strain and cool.
Mix 3 cups orange juice, 3 cups pineapple juice, 1 cup lemon juice.
Mix together the syrup, tea and juices and add 1½ quarts ginger ale at serving time.

Veranda Punch

Boil ½ cup water and ½ cup sugar for 5 minutes. Steep 1 cup tea. Cool each.
Press juice from 3 lemons and 2 oranges.
Mix together and add 1 pint ginger ale and 1 pint soda water at serving time.
Garnish the punch bowl with orange and lemon slices.

Friendship Tea

3 packages Tang
⅛ cup instant tea
1 package lemonade mix
½ cup sugar
1 teaspoon cloves
1 teaspoon cinnamon
   (powdered)

Mix. To use put 2–3 teaspoons in a cup and fill with boiling water.

For the Punch Bowl

Boil 1 cup sugar and 2 cups water. Cool.
At serving time mix the ingredients.
2 6-ounce cans frozen orange juice
2 6-ounce cans frozen grapefruit juice
2 28-ounce bottles ginger ale
⅔ cup grenadine (purchase at grocer's)

Lemon-Orange Concentrate

Grate rinds and squeeze juice from 3 lemons and 4 oranges. Strain juices if desired.

To 8 cups white sugar add 1½ quarts boiling water and 2 ounces citric acid, which is available at drugstores. Cool.

Mix the syrup and the juices.
Bottle and refrigerate.
Good mixed with water or as a base in a punch bowl.

Cranberry Punch

1 package cranberries
3 quarts water
2 cinnamon sticks

Cook and put through sieve.
(Bottled juice could be used instead.)

Add juice of 6 oranges and 2 lemons,
2 cups sugar.
Heat all to boiling point.
Add ginger ale or lemon-lime soda at serving time.

Dandelion Drink (not wine)

Pour 4 quarts boiling water on 1 quart dandelion blossoms. Let stand 24 hours. Strain.
To another 4 quarts water add 4 cups sugar and 4 lemons that have been thinly sliced. Boil 5 minutes, add dandelion liquid, return to boil and seal in sterile jars.

Homemade Rhubarb Juice

3½ quarts (18 cups) washed,
   cut rhubarb
12 cups hot water
2 cups sugar
½ teaspoon red color

Simmer rhubarb and water for about 40 minutes.
Strain through sieve and put on to heat.
Add sugar and coloring. When it boils it may be bottled in sterile jars.
When making punch add equal parts of pineapple juice, a tray of ice and red and green cherries.
Yield: 4 32-ounce bottles

Note: You can use the last of the crop for this.

Salads and
Salad Dressings

Sauerkraut Salad

32 ounces sauerkraut
(drained)
1 cup celery
1 green pepper (diced)
1 sweet pepper
1 pimiento
1 cup sugar
⅓ cup salad oil
⅓ cup white vinegar
¼ cup water
1 teaspoon salt
onion

Mix all ingredients and let stand for one hour.

Canned Bean Salad

Clean and cut a 6 quart basket of beans. Cook until tender but not mushy. Drain and save liquid and add enough water to make 4 cups.
Add:
1½ cups sugar
¼ teaspoon dry mustard
1½ cups vinegar
½ teaspoons turmeric
1 teaspoon salt

Bring to a boil. Pack drained hot beans in jars. Cover with boiling syrup and seal. To use, drain off liquid. Add onions and sour cream to serve. Also hard boiled eggs can be added.

Old Fashioned Bean Salad

1 quart plain canned green
and yellow beans
1 onion
1 teaspoon vinegar
1 teaspoon sugar
salt and pepper

Let all stand 2–3 hours. At serving time add:
¾ cup *sour* cream, 2 hard cooked eggs.

Potato Salad (cold)

1 quart boiled diced potatoes
1 pint cabbage and celery
2 hard boiled eggs
½ teaspoon salt
a little pepper

Mix well and add boiled dressing.

Good for a picnic!

Dressing
Melt 1 heaping tablespoon
    butter
1 egg, well beaten
½ cup vinegar
1 cup sour cream
½ teaspoon mustard
½ cup sugar

Boil until thick.

Cabbage Salad

1 onion, chopped fine
1 small head cabbage, shredded
Add: 1 cup sugar, 1 teaspoon salt and mix.
Heat: ½ cup vinegar to boiling piont.
Add: ¾ cup oil (may use less)
1 teaspoon celery seed
1 teaspoon prepared mustard
⅛–¼ teaspoon turmeric
Add all to shredded cabbage.
Store 3–4 hours before serving.
Options: Add green and red pepper, shredded carrots for color.

Salad of Greens *(dandelion, endive or spinach)*

Dressing (for approximately
    4 cups greens)
3 slices bacon, cut and fry
2 tablespoons flour, blend
    into hot fried bacon
Reduce heat and add
2–4 tablespoons sugar
¼ cup vinegar—blend well
½–¾ cup cream (milk or
    water if calorie conscious)

When it comes to boil add greens and 2–3 hard cooked eggs. An egg shredded over top is a nice garnish. Serve at once. Do not allow to fully wilt.

2 Week Cole Slaw

1 medium cabbage
1 Spanish onion
1 green pepper
1 cup cider vinegar
1 cup white sugar
1 teaspoon salt
1 teaspoon mustard salt
1 teaspoon celery salt

Shred vegetables, mix with dressing and store 24 hours before using.

Hot Potato Salad

4 cups hot diced potatoes
1 cup chopped celery
1 teaspoon chopped parsley
1 onion, chopped
½ teaspoon pepper
2 tablespoons salad oil or lard
1½ teaspoons salt
1 tablespoon flour
⅛ cup vinegar
⅛ cup sugar
⅔ cup water

Fry chopped onion in hot lard until light brown. Add flour and blend. Then add salt, sugar, vinegar and water. Bring to a boil, stirring constantly. Pour dressing over the potatoes. Mix in celery and parsley. Sprinkle with pepper and paprika and serve hot.
Serves 6.
Good on a cold winter's night with fried ham.

Gelatin Salad

1 package lemon gelatin, 1 teaspoon sugar, 1 cup boiling water
Mix and let stand until cooled but not jellied.
Add: 1 cup milk, 1 cup little marshmallows, 2 tablespoons salad dressing.
Let stand until starting to set. Add 1 can fruit cocktail, well drained. Stir in
gelatin and let set.

Orange Gelatin Salad

Dissolve 3 ounces orange gelatin in 2 cups boiling water. Add juice from 1 can
pineapple tidbits.

Add 8 ounces cream cheese. Beat until well blended, then add:

1 cup miniature marshmallows
½ cup salad dressing

Blend. Let cool until almost set, then stir in pineapple and 1 can mandarin
oranges (well drained), ¼ cup maraschino cherries cut up, ¼ cup walnuts.

Pour into mold. For added attraction dissolve one package colored gelatin, pour
into mold and let harden before adding above salad. Delicious!

Cranberry Salad

1 package cranberries
  (1 pound)
4 apples
2 oranges *or* ½ cup
  crushed pineapple
2 cups sugar
3 packages raspberry gelatin
3 cups hot water
3 cups cold water
½ cup nuts

Wash and grind cranberries in food chopper.
Pare and core apples and chop or grind fine.
Add chopped oranges, nuts and sugar.
Dissolve gelatin in hot water. Add cold water.
When cool and beginning to congeal, add
salad mixture. Makes a very large salad.

California Salad

1 cup sour cream
1 cup marshmallows
1 cup crushed pineapple
  (drained)
1 cup shredded coconut
1 can mandarin orange
  segments

Mix together and let set a few hours.

½ cup green and red seedless grapes may be added.

Orange Banana Salad

Dissolve:
1 6-ounce package banana-orange gelatin
⅓ cup sugar in 2 cups boiling water
⅛ teaspoon salt
Add:
½ cup orange juice
1 teaspoon grated orange rind
1¼ cups cold water
Measure 2 cups and chill to slightly thickened.
Fold in:
1 cup diced orange sections, 1 banana sliced

Spoon into 6 cup mold and chill until almost firm. Meanwhile chill remaining gelatin to slightly thickened. Whip ½ cup cream and fold into gelatin. Spoon over gelatin in mold. Chill until firm.
Serves 8–10.

Fruit Cream Dressing *Serve in small bowl.*

3 tablespoons sugar
2 tablespoons flour
2 eggs
2 tablespoons vinegar
1 cup pear or pineapple juice
1 lemon rind and juice

Mix in order given, and cook over boiling water until thick. Before serving add 1 cup cream whipped stiff, or whipped topping substitute.

Festive Party Salad

6 ounces lime gelatin
2 cups boiling water
2 cups cold water
1 teaspoon unflavored gelatin
11-ounce can mandarin
   oranges
4-ounce package white cream
   cheese, room temperature
¼ cup chopped walnuts or
   pecans
1 cup finely chopped inner
   celery stalks

In medium sized bowl soak the unflavored gelatin in ¼ cup cold water for 5 minutes. Add the lime gelatin and then the boiling water. Stir well. Add the remaining 1¾ cups cold water. Stir and chill until partially set.

Cream the cheese in a small bowl, shape into small balls and then roll in the nuts. Fold the balls, the drained orange sections and celery into the jelly that is set to a heavy syrup stage. Turn into a mold. Chill till set.

Tuna Salad

1 cup tomato juice
¼ cup mayonnaise
2 packages unflavored gelatin
Heat tomato juice and add soaked gelatin to heated juice and let set.
Add mayonnaise to tomato-gelatin mixture when partially cooked.
2 cans tuna or 1 large can salmon
3 tablespoons hot dog relish
chopped onion (small)
Mix with gelatin and pour in mold.
This salad is ideal for a fish mold.

Lemon-Lime Gelatin Salad

1 package lemon gelatin
1 package lime gelatin
2 cups boiling water
2 cups cold water
20 ounces crushed pineapple
2 cups mini marshmallows
2 or 3 bananas
2 ounces slivered almonds
   (optional)

Dissolve gelatin in boiling water, stir in cold water. Chill partially. Drain pineapple, reserving juice for another use. Fold in pineapple, sliced bananas, marshmallows and almonds into gelatin. Pour into 7x12 inch pan. Chill until firm. Orange gelatin may be used as a substitute.

Whipped Cream Topping for Gelatin Salads

½ cup sugar
3 tablespoons flour
1 cup pineapple juice
1 egg, slightly beaten
1 tablespoon butter
½ cup whipping cream or
    whipped topping
¼ cup shredded cheese
2 tablespoons Parmesan
    cheese

Combine sugar, flour in saucepan. Stir in juice and egg. Cook over low heat until thickened. Add butter. Cool. Fold into whipped cream and use to frost gelatin salads. Sprinkle with cheese.

Vegetable Salad

3 packages lemon gelatin mixed with 3 cups boiling water. Let set until it begins to jell.
Then add:
1 cup grated carrot, ½ cup chopped celery, ½ cup chopped green pepper, 1 small chopped onion, 1¼ cups mayonnaise, 1 pound cottage cheese

Mix and put in mold.

Cranberry-Raspberry Salad

1 3-ounce package raspberry
    gelatin
1 3-ounce package lemon
    gelatin
1½ cups boiling water
1 10-ounce package frozen
    raspberries
1 16-ounce can whole
    cranberry sauce
1 7-ounce bottle lemon-lime
    soda

Mix gelatin with boiling water. Add frozen berries, breaking lumps with fork. Add cranberries. Chill until partially set. Slowly add soda. Chill firmly.

Cream Cheese Salad (3 color)

Colorful—and good too!

1 3-ounce package lime gelatin
Dissolve in 2 cups boiling water.
Cool until syrupy. Then add 2 cups pineapple which has been drained. Pour into 2 quart mold. Set in refrigerator until firm.

In the meantime, dissolve 1 tablespoon unflavored gelatin in ½ cup cold water. Heat 1 cup pineapple juice and add the gelatin and stir until dissolved. Remove from heat and cool. Mash up 6 ounces cream cheese and blend into the juice with beater. Then stir into that 1 cup whipped cream. Pour this on top of lime gelatin and let set until firm.

Dissolve 1 package red gelatin in 1¾ cups boiling water. Cool well and pour over firm cheese layer. Set until all is firm. Serve on glass plate and decorate with whipped cream and mayonnaise.

Variation: Sprinkle with grated coconut, nuts or grated cheese.

Coleslaw Parfait Salad

1 package lemon gelatin
1 cup hot water
½ cup salad dressing
½ cup cold water
2 tablespoons vinegar
1½ cups finely shredded
    cabbage
½ cup radish slices
½ cup diced celery
2–4 tablespoons diced green
    pepper
½ teaspoon salt
1 tablespoon diced onion

Dissolve jello in hot water. Blend in Miracle Whip, cold water, vinegar and salt. Chill until partially set. Beat until fluffy. Add vegetables. Pour into mold. Chill and set.

Fruited Cheese Salad

3 cups creamed style cottage cheese
1 quart frozen whipped topping, thawed
1 3-ounce package each orange and pineapple gelatin
1 can pineapple tidbits (drained)
1 small can mandarin oranges (drained)

In mixer blend cottage cheese and whipped topping. Stir in dry jello. Fold in pineapple tidbits and oranges and put in mold. Chill several hours.
Serves 12.

Chicken Salad

2 cups cooked chicken, cubed
1 cup pineapple tidbits
1 cup orange sections
1 cup chopped celery
2 tablespoons orange juice
1 teaspoon marjoram
½ teaspoon salt
1 teaspoon vinegar

Mix above and put in refrigerator for 1 hour before serving. Add ¼ cup mayonnaise and mix.

Mexicali Salad Ring

1 can red kidney beans
1 can mandarin oranges
½ cup chopped onion
¼ cup chopped parsley
¼ cup salad oil
2 tablespoons cider vinegar
1 teaspoon sugar
½ teaspoon salt
lettuce

Drain kidney beans and orange segments. Toss onion with parsley in a small bowl. Mix salad oil, vinegar, sugar and salt in a cup. Line a serving bowl with lettuce. Spoon beans in a ring around edge and mandarin oranges next to beans. Pile onion mixture in center. Drizzle dressing over.
This is delicious and something different.

Salads and Salad Dressings

Marinated Carrot Salad

1 pound carrots,
  diagonally sliced
1 medium onion, thinly sliced
1 medium green pepper,
  in strips
½ 10-ounce can tomato soup
½ cup sugar
½ cup salad oil
½ teaspoon dry mustard
⅓ cup vinegar
¼ teaspoon salt
¼ teaspoon pepper

Cook carrots just until tender, about 8 minutes. (Do not overcook.) Drain. Add onion rings and green pepper strips. Whip remaining ingredients until blended; pour over vegetables. Marinate several hours or overnight in refrigerator. To serve, lift vegetables out of dressing and place in lettuce-lined serving dish. Serves 6–8.
Salad and salad dressing keep well in refrigerator.

Horseradish Salad

2 cups beets, shredded (scant)
2 cups liquid from beets and
  water
1 package gelatin
5 tablespoons white sugar
1¼ teaspoons salt
1 tablespoon horseradish
1 tablespoon lemon juice

Mix all ingredients and serve in a bowl.

The world is composed of takers and givers.
The takers may eat better,
but the givers sleep better.

Far East Fruit Plate

1 can (20–ounce) pineapple
   chunks
1 can (11–ounce) mandarin
   oranges (drained)
2 large bananas, sliced
½ cup chopped dates
2 tablespoons vinegar
¼ cup salad oil
1 teaspoon curry powder
¼ teaspoon salt
2 pounds cottage cheese
½ cup chopped salted peanuts
   or almonds
Crisp salad greens

Drain pineapple reserving ½ cup syrup. Combine pineapple and next 3 ingredients in large bowl. Combine reserved syrup with next 4 ingredients in jar, cover and shake well. Pour over fruit and marinate ½ hour. Arrange greens in bowl. Spoon cheese into greens and top with fruit mixture. Sprinkle with peanuts. Serves 6. This is a good salad with an Oriental dinner.

Quick French Dressing

½ cup sugar
1 teaspoon paprika
1 teaspoon salt
¼ cup cider vinegar
⅓ cup catsup
¼ cup salad oil
juice of ½ lemon

Put all ingredients into a 20–ounce jar with lid and shake well. Serve.

St. Anthony Salad Dressing

1 cup catsup
1 cup salad oil
½ cup grated cheese
   (cheddar preferred)
2 onions, chopped
1 cup white sugar
½ cup vinegar

Mix and shake in quart jar.
Good for a tossed salad of lettuce alone or a variety of greens and crispy vegetables. This dressing will keep in refrigerator for a few weeks. Delicious!

Hot Mustard *(uncooked)*

1 cup flour
¾ cup brown sugar
¾ teaspoon salt
5 tablespoons *dry* mustard
5 tablespoons prepared
   mustard
1 cup vinegar

Mix all together and store in jar.

Russian Salad Dressing

1½ cup salad dressing
   (Miracle Whip)
¼ cup catsup
4 tablespoons sweet pickle
   relish
½ teaspoon garlic salt
½ teaspoon pepper

Mix well.
Add 1 cup evaporated milk.
This keeps a long time in refrigerator.

French Dressing

1 10-ounce can tomato soup
½ cup white sugar
½ cup vinegar
½ cup salad oil
1½ teaspoons prepared
   mustard
⅛ teaspoon Worcestershire
   sauce
1½ teaspoons salt
1½ teaspoons paprika
1 teaspoon pepper
a shake of garlic salt
a shake of onion salt

Shake all together and store in refrigerator.

Mustard (boiled)

1 egg, beaten
¼ cup sugar
1 teaspoon cornstarch
4 teaspoons dry mustard
1 cup vinegar
salt

Mix all together and boil.

Boiled Salad Dressing

3 eggs
5 tablespoons sugar
2 dessert spoons flour
1 teaspoon mustard
1 cup water
1 teaspoon salt
pinch of pepper
1 cup vinegar
    (cider vinegar preferred)

Mix all ingredients and set on to boil, stirring continually until it thickens. Take off heat and cool.

Can be used warm, or put in little jars. Keeps well in refrigerator.

Mayonnaise

1 cup white sugar
2 eggs
¼ teaspoon salt, pepper
2 teaspoons dry mustard
2 teaspoons flour
butter size of an egg
¾ cup vinegar
¾ cup water

Mix all together and cook over a slow fire. To use: mix equal parts of cream with mayonnaise.

Soups

Cream of Bean Soup

2 cups yellow beans soaked overnight. Cook slowly until very soft and mushy.
Put through fruit press.

Add:
1 quart rich milk
salt to taste.

Fry:
½ cup celery
½ cup grated carrot
¼ cup finely minced onion
2 slices lean side bacon
until tender but not real soft.

Add to beans and milk.
Heat to scalding point and serve with toasted bread cubes, or crackers.

Wiener Potato Soup

1 cup chopped onion
3 cups peeled, diced potatoes
3 cups boiling water

Cook until very tender. May be put through sieve if you like.

Add to potato mixture (potato water included):
4 chicken bouillon cubes
3 tablespoons butter
1 cup milk
1 cup light cream
1 teaspoon salt
¼ teaspoon pepper

Stir well and heat to *almost* boiling.
Cut ½ pound wieners into thin slices and add a generous spoonful to each bowl
of piping hot soup.
Serves 6.

Hamburger Soup *(a real family favorite)*

1½ pounds hamburger
    (lean ground beef)
3 eggs
1 tablespoon flour
1¼ teaspoons salt
1 medium onion—diced
Mix the above and make into round little meatballs,
put them into:
2 quarts water
1 bay leaf
3–4 potatoes, diced
½ cup chopped onion
Cook until meat and vegetables are done, about 1 hour. Add salt to taste.

To 1 slightly beaten egg add enough flour to make fairly stiff dough. Drop by small spoonfuls into hot soup. Add a bit of chopped parsley. Cover and let dumplings cook for 10 minutes. Add ½ cup sweet cream and just bring to a boil *or* remove from heat and add ½ cup sour cream.

Smoked Sausage Potato Soup

4 large potatoes—peeled
1 pound smoked sausage
1 tablespoon onion finely
    chopped (optional)
¼ teaspoon salt
milk
parsley

Cut sausage in ¼ inch pieces; put into 3 quart pan with 2 inches water. Cube potatoes; put in pan with sausage; add onion and ¼ teaspoon salt.

Cover and bring to boil. Cook over medium heat stirring frequently to stop sticking and burning bottom of pan. Cook about 20 to 30 minutes until potatoes are soft. Cover with milk; add a few sprinkles of dried parsley or fresh chopped (optional). Cover and let stand 5 minutes. It should be very thick.
Serves 4–6. Old family recipe.

Turkey or Chicken Soup

Save all the bones, plus any part that wasn't served such as neck, stomach, heart and liver, etc. Put into large kettle, fill at least half full with water, add some celery leaves, an onion, favorite seasoning and simmer slowly several hours; add more water if necessary; strain through sieve. Now you have a rich broth.

To broth add mixture of vegetables and some leftover turkey or chicken cut fine and ½ cup alphabet macaroni; or just noodles and meat chunks for noodle soup.

Chinese Soup

1 package Lipton's Chicken
    Noodle Soup
**Prepare as directed on
package.**
Add:
½ cup frozen peas
1 can mushrooms

Drizzle 1 well beaten egg into the soup. Cut up green onion tops can also be added.

Delicious!

Butter Balls or Rivels

2 tablespoons butter
6 eggs
6 tablespoons flour
¼ teaspoon salt

Beat butter until soft. Beat and add eggs. Stir in the flour and salt. May be stored in refrigerator until ready for use.

Drop from spoon into the simmering soup and cook for about 5 minutes. Serves 6.

Use any meat broth, especially good with chicken or beef.

Chicken Noodle Soup

chicken
cinnamon
parsley
bay leaves
whole ginger
onion

Cut chicken in serving pieces; cover with cold water in fairly large pot. Simmer for 3 hours; add spices for another half hour.

Cook noodles in this broth.

Oyster Soup

Always served for the big families on Grandpa's birthday and supper on
Christmas Day.

Heat milk—about 1½ cups per person.
When hot add oysters—3 or 4 per person or as many more as you can afford.
Season with salt, pepper and butter.
Heat until oysters are hot and curl a bit.

✓ Bread Soup

1 tablespoon butter
2 slices bread, cut into
   ¾ inch squares
pinch of salt
½ cup (or more) boiling water
¼ cup cream

Melt butter and add bread cubes. After the
bread is browned, put it into a dish and add
salt, water and cream.

Bread soup is easy to digest and is a favorite
food after the children have an upset stomach
or when they are sick.

Butter Soup

1 onion
salt
2 bay leaves
4 small potatoes
4 pepper kernels

Cover with water and cook for 1 hour.

Add dumplings (see below) and cook for a few
more minutes until dumplings are cooked.

Add cream and 1 teaspoon butter.

Angel Food Dumplings

1 cup all-purpose flour
2½ teaspoons baking powder
¼ teaspoon salt
⅓ cup milk
1 egg

Sift dry ingredients. Beat egg; add milk, then
add to dry ingredients.

Drop by spoon into boiling stew.
Let rise until puffed, about 5 minutes; then
cover and cook gently for about 15 minutes.
(Good on sauerkraut.)

Special European Mennonite Dishes

Special European Mennonite Dishes

Many Mennonites left their German-Prussian homelands to escape persecution and build a new life in the Russian Ukraine from 1789–1797. Empress Catherine II of Russia invited them, promising religious freedom. They prospered, built churches, schools and huge farms and businesses. However, rulers changed, promises were broken and they were oppressed and suffered with others of Russia.

Those wishing to emigrate were forced to leave homes, possessions and even family behind. Settling primarily in the West they brought their German–type cooking with the influence of the central European countries where they had sojourned. We share some of these in this section.

Borscht

2 pounds beef with bone
1 large onion
1 carrot
1 red beet
3 potatoes
½ cabbage head, shredded
bunch parsley and dill
salt, hot red pepper or
    peppercorns to taste
1 can tomatoes

Simmer meat in 2 quarts salted water till meat is done (about 2 hours). Then add 1 can tomatoes chopped. Tie onion, parsley and dill in cheesecloth (also pepper). Add shredded vegetables (carrot may be left whole and removed before serving) and simmer for 1 hour. If soup lacks body, a can of tomato soup may be added. Taste for seasoning. A spoon of sour cream may be added to each serving.

Serve with Fleisch Piroschky (page 168) or Rollkuchen (page 173).

Kielke *(homemade macaroni)*

3 cups flour
2 teaspoons salt
3 eggs
½ cup milk

Mix all ingredients to make fairly hard dough. Knead well. Roll out very thin, and flour both sides. Cut dough into 1 inch strips. Place 2 strips together and cut in fine pieces. Cook in boiling salt water for a few minutes. Serve with fried onions and cream sauce.

Cream Sauce
½ cup cream
2 tablespoons melted butter

Melt butter, browning slightly. Add cream and heat to boiling point. Pour over kielke.

Piramanie *(meat pockets)*

3 eggs, 3 tablespoons water, enough flour to make a stiff dough. Roll dough fairly thin and cut into 2 inch squares. Fill with cooked ground beef seasoned with salt, pepper and grated onion. Take two corners to make a triangle and press open edges together very firmly. Cook in boiling salted water or beef broth for 10 minutes. Drain. Pour browned butter over to serve.

Garlic is not only a food but also a very good herb for medicinal uses. It aids digestion, relieves dyspepsia and colic; it acts as an intestinal antiseptic and blood purifier. It destroys round and thread worms. It is a good nerve tonic and very beneficial in colds and coughs. It is very rich in vitamins and minerals.

Fleisch Piroschky (meat buns)

½ cup warm water
1 package dry yeast
1 tablespoon sugar
1 cup scalded milk
½ cup shortening
1½ teaspoons salt
3 cups flour

Scald and cool milk, add yeast which has been dissolved in warm water plus sugar. Add remaining ingredients to make soft dough as for rolls. Let rise. Pinch off pieces of dough and flatten into rounds with hands. Place 1 tablespoon of meat filling on dough and form into an oblong bun. Place on well greased cookie sheet and bake at 350° for 25–30 minutes or until golden brown.

Meat Filling
1 onion, chopped
½ pound ground leftover beef
½ teaspoon salt
1 or 2 hard boiled eggs
    (optional)
leftover gravy or sour cream

Saute onion gently until yellow. Add to ground meat and eggs which have also been put through food chopper. Add salt and enough gravy or sour cream to moisten. Instead of gravy or cream combine with a cup of mashed potato. Makes the filling very light and fluffy.

Schmoor Kohl (stewed cabbage with fruit)

12 cups chopped white
    cabbage
2 cups chopped dried apples
15 prunes
Put above ingredients in heavy
saucepan and add:
¾ cup water
½ cup oil
2½ teaspoons salt
⅓ cup white sugar

Cook several minutes, then cover and simmer 1½ to 2 hours. If fruit is very sour add a little more sugar.

Try a dash of kindness with
a pinch of love today. Top it off with a bit of
cheerfulness and add a touch of goodwill.
See how much better the day can be!

Bubbat *(sausage square)*

1 package yeast
½ cup warm water
1 teaspoon sugar
½ cup milk
3 tablespoons butter
2 eggs, beaten
1 teaspoon salt
flour to make soft dough
    (approximately 2½ to 3
    cups)
bacon
smoked pork sausage

Combine yeast, warm water and sugar. Let rise 10 minutes. Heat milk and butter slightly. Mix with eggs, salt, yeast mixture. Add enough flour to make a soft dough that can barely be stirred with a spoon. Line a 9x9 inch pan with bacon strips. Spoon half of dough into pan. Arrange smoked pork sausage cut in 2 inch pieces over all. Put remaining dough on top. Let rise 1 hour. Bake at 375° for 45 minutes.

Apple Moos

3–4 cups peeled chopped
    apple
2 cups water
4 cups milk
2½ tablespoons cornstarch
    mixed in a little cold water
¼ cup sugar
few grains salt

Cook apples in 2 cups water until soft. Meanwhile bring to boil over low heat the milk and salt. Add cornstarch mixture and cook for about 10 minutes until the taste of raw starch disappears. Add ¼ to ½ cup sugar to taste. Remove from heat and add the cooked apples stirring constantly, or mixture becomes lumpy. If moos is too thick, thin with a little more milk. Plums or dried fruits may be used in place of apples.

Glums Vareneki *(cottage cheese filled noodles)*

1 cup milk
2 eggs
2¾ cups flour
1 teaspoon salt

Sift flour and salt. Add milk and eggs beating well to make a medium soft dough. Roll out fairly thin and cut in 4 inch squares or cut out with round cutter.

Cottage Cheese (Glums)
Filling
2 cups fine dry cottage cheese
1 teaspoon salt
2 egg yolks

Mix well. Fill squares or rounds with glums filling and pinch edges well to seal. Cook in boiling water for 5 minutes. Serve with fried onions or cream gravy or browned butter.

Zwetschen Knoedel

6 medium potatoes
1 tablespoon butter
1 egg, beaten
2 cups flour
1 teaspoon salt
40 fresh plums (German prune plums are best)

Cook potatoes, then peel and mash while warm, add butter, salt and egg, mixing well. Knead in enough flour to make a soft dough that can be rolled out. Cut off pieces large enough to cover one plum, rolling and sealing edges. When all knoedel are made drop gently into boiling salted water, stirring gently at first so they will not stick to saucepan. Cook until fruit is done (about 10 or 15 minutes). Take out one at a time with slotted spoon and roll in fine bread crumbs and melted shortening. Serve with sugar and sour cream.

Really different and so good!

Apple Strudel

3 cups all-purpose flour
½ teaspoon salt
1 egg
½ cup warm water (or more if needed)
1 tablespoon salad oil
1 tablespoon shortening (melted)
8 apples
½ cup sugar
cinnamon to taste

Pour flour and salt in bowl. Beat egg and warm water and add the salad oil if desired. (I find this makes dough easier to stretch.) Work liquid into flour to make a soft dough that does not stick to board, kneading and rolling well for at least 10 minutes. Cover with a bowl and allow to rest for 30 minutes. Spread a clean cloth on card table. Flour. Roll dough as thin as possible and then stretch with hands until very very thin and at least as large as the table and hanging over the sides. Brush with melted shortening. Sprinkle with peeled shredded apple, sugar and cinnamon. Lift cloth and roll up as a jelly roll. Fry in electric fry pan in a little shortening until golden brown.

Variation: Sprinkle apples with cottage cheese.
Roll up and bake at 350–375° for 1 hour.

*Let the other fellow talk occasionally,
you can't learn much listening to yourself!*

Christmas Cookies *A tradition at our house.*

Cream together:
3 cups white sugar
3 cups corn syrup
3 eggs
½ cup butter
20 drops oil of lemon
 (from the drugstore)

Sift together:
1 teaspoon soda
1 teaspoon baking powder
2 teaspoons spices (cloves and
 cinnamon to taste)
1 teaspoon salt
4 cups flour (first amount)

Mix together and then continue to add flour to make a dough that can be rolled. It will take about 5 more cups. Roll out and cut into rounds. A scalloped cutter may be used. Press ½ teaspoon jam on top and cover with another round. Press together. Bake at 375° about 12 minutes. Best if made several days before using. May be iced after they have been stored.

Nusskuchen

½ cup butter
½ cup sugar
3 egg yolks
1½ cups all-purpose flour
2 teaspoons baking powder
½ teaspoon salt
2 tablespoons milk
rind of 1 lemon

Filbert Filling
2 cups finely ground
 filbert nuts
3 egg whites
1 cup sugar
few drops bitter almond oil

Mix all ingredients for cake and roll on floured board ¼ inch thick.
For filling add nuts to remaining ingredients. Mix well. Spread filling on cake and roll as a jelly roll. Bake at 350° about 1 hour. Dust with powdered sugar. Should mellow for several days.

The discovery of a new dish makes more for the happiness of man than the discovery of a star.

Hungarian Cheesecake

4 tablespoons butter
2 egg yolks
⅛ teaspoon salt
2 tablespoons lemon juice
1½ cups sifted flour
1 teaspoon baking powder
2–3 tablespoons cold water

Cream butter. Beat in egg yolks, salt and lemon juice. Add sifted dry ingredients and water to make a smooth dough. Pat out to ¼ inch thick into large pie plate or spring-form pan.

Filling
1 cup dry cottage cheese
1 cup thick sour cream
⅓ cup sugar
½ teaspoon salt
3 eggs, well beaten
1 teaspoon grated lemon rind
1 cup crushed pineapple, drained
½ cup seedless raisins or cherries (whole or chopped)

1 egg white, slightly beaten

Press cheese through sieve (or use very fine cheese) and measure. Add sour cream, sugar, salt, eggs and lemon rind, beating well. Brush dough with egg white, sprinkle evenly with pineapple and raisins or cherries. Add cottage cheese mixture. Bake at 450° for 10 minutes. Reduce heat to 350° and bake 20 minutes or until browned. Serve cold.

Fastnacht Doughnuts

1 cup milk
2 eggs, separated
1½ cups raisins
¼ cup butter
2 teaspoons salt
1 package dry yeast
¼ cup water
2 teaspoons sugar
1 teaspoon lemon rind
2½ cups flour

Dissolve yeast in the ¼ cup warm water in which the 2 teaspoons sugar have been dissolved. Set aside for at least 10 minutes. Scald the milk and add salt, butter and egg yolks when it has cooled to lukewarm. Beat egg whites until stiff. Sift flour into bowl and make well in center. Add yeast mixture and milk mixture and stir to mix. Stir in raisins and rind and fold in egg whites. Let rise for 1 hour. Heat fat in fryer to 425°. Drop batter in by teaspoonfuls. Sprinkle with sifted powdered sugar when cooled.

Two things are bad for the heart—
running up stairs, and running down people.

Rollkuchen

4 cups flour
2 teaspoons baking powder
1 teaspoon salt
1 cup sour cream
1 cup milk
4 eggs

Sift dry ingredients, make well and add rest of ingredients. Mix well with hands. Roll out on floured board and cut in 2x4 inch strips. Fry in deep hot fat until golden brown on one side, turn and fry on other side. If you roll them quite thin they are very crisp. If a softer rollkuchen is preferred do not roll as thin. Serve with watermelon or borscht. (These may be cut into diamonds and twisted through a center slit. Fry and sprinkle with powdered sugar when cool.)

Piroschky (fruit)

2 cups flour
1 teaspoon baking powder
1 teaspoon salt
1 tablespoon lard
½ cup milk
½ cup cream
1 egg

Sift dry ingredients, cut in lard, add slightly beaten egg, milk and cream. If dough is too soft to handle, add a little more flour. Roll out on floured board, cut in squares and fill with apples, gooseberries, or any other fruit. Top with 1 tablespoon sugar (more if you like it sweeter*). Fold opposite corners over and seal. Bake at 400° for 25 minutes.

*Mix 1 cup sugar with 2 tablespoons flour and sprinkle on fruit.

Don't judge a man by the house he lives in—lizards and rats are often known to inhabit the grandest structures.

Paska (Easter bread)

3 packages yeast
4 cups sugar
16 eggs
1 cup butter
1 teaspoon salt
3 cups scalded milk
8 cups flour
Juice and rind of 1 lemon

Soften yeast in 1 cup warm water and 2 teaspoons sugar. Beat eggs well, add sugar gradually and beat until dissolved. Sift flour and salt. Make well in flour and add cooled scalded milk. Stir and add the egg mixture. Beat well. Add softened butter and fruit juice and rind. Now add yeast mixture and knead adding more flour to make firm dough. Let rise in a warm place until double in bulk. Grease honey pails and fill ⅓ with dough. Let rise until light. Bake at 325° for 1 hour. Makes 12 paska. Serve with Cheese Spread (recipe below) if desired.

Cheese Spread for Paska

4 cups cottage cheese
yolks of 9 hard cooked eggs
1 cup cream
1 cup butter
1 cup sugar
1 teaspoon grated lemon rind
1 tablespoon lemon juice

Press cheese and egg yolks through sieve. (May be whirled in blender.) Bring cream to a boil and cool. Cream butter and sugar and add rest of ingredients. Mix well. This may now be used as a spread for paska. (May be placed in a cheesecloth lined sieve and allowed to drain.)

Rosinen Stritzel (raisin bread)

3 cups scalded milk
3 cups flour
½ pound shortening
¼ pound butter
1½ pounds raisins
1½ tablespoons salt
2 eggs, well beaten
2 packages dry yeast, dissolved
    as directed
about 7½ cups flour

When milk is cooled add 3 cups flour, eggs, salt, dissolved yeast and work in shortening and butter by hand. Now add raisins and rest of flour to make a fairly stiff dough. Let rise until double in bulk. Shape into loaves and place in bread pans which have been well greased. Bake at 350° for one hour.

Zwieback

2 cups scalded milk
1 cup warm water
2 teaspoons salt
4 tablespoons sugar
1 package yeast
1 cup butter and shortening
8–10 cups flour

Scald milk, add shortening, salt and 4 tablespoons sugar. Put yeast in a small bowl, add 2 teaspoons sugar and 1 cup warm water. Set in a warm place until spongy. Add yeast mixture to warm milk. Mix well and stir in flour gradually. Knead dough until very soft and smooth. Cover and let rise in warm place until double in bulk. Pinch off small balls of dough the size of a small egg. Place 1 inch apart on greased pan. Put a smaller bun on top of each bun and press with thumb. Let rise again until double in bulk (1 hour). Bake at 400–425° for 15–20 minutes. Yield: 4 dozen

Fruit Platz or Coffee Cake

3 tablespoons butter
3 tablespoons cream
1 egg
¼ cup sugar
dash of salt
1 cup all-purpose flour
2 teaspoons baking powder
1 teaspoon vanilla
fruit

Cream butter, cream egg, sugar, and salt all together. Add flour, baking powder and vanilla to make soft dough. Press into a greased 9x9x2 inch pan. Cover with sliced fruit: plums, cherries, apples, apricots.
Top with crumb mixture: rub together ½ cup flour, ½ cup sugar, 3 tablespoons butter. Bake at 375° for 30 minutes or until done. Serve plain or with whipped cream. Good hot or cold.

Give a pat on the back today.
Its effect goes on and on—
like that of a pebble thrown into water.

Pluskie (*sweet buns*)

2 packages yeast
1 cup warm water or
    potato water
1 tablespoon sugar
2 cups scalded milk
1½ cups fat (½ cup shortening,
    ½ cup margarine,
    ½ cup butter)
2 cups white sugar
6 eggs
1 teaspoon salt
2 tablespoons vanilla
all-purpose flour
    (8–10 cups, approximately)

Dissolve yeast in water with 1 tablespoon sugar. Let stand in warm place until spongy. Beat eggs and sugar until thick and light. Scald milk and cool to lukewarm. Add yeast mixture, egg mixture, fats, salt and vanilla. Gradually add flour, first beating with spoon then kneading until dough can be handled. Let rise in warm place until double in bulk. Pinch off small pieces of dough (the size of a golf ball) and place 1 inch apart on greased baking pan. Let rise again until double in bulk. Bake at 375° until golden brown.
These taste much like paska (Easter bread) (recipe on page 174) but are not quite as rich.

Raised Piroschky (*sweet*)

½ cup warm water
1 package yeast
1 cup scalded milk
½ cup sugar
½ cup shortening
1½ teaspoons salt
3 cups flour

Use either dried fruit, cooked and sweetened to taste until consistency of jam. Fresh fruit may also be used.
Scald and cool milk, add yeast which has been dissolved in warm water and 1 teaspoon sugar. Add remaining ingredients to make a soft dough as for rolls. Let rise. Roll out to ¼ inch thick. Place dabs of fruit on dough, far enough from the edge that dough may be folded over it. Cut with round cutter into half circles. The straight side is fold of the dough. Set on greased pan folded side down. Pinch edges well. Bake at 350° for 25 to 30 minutes.

This dough may also be used as a base for fruit platz. Press into well greased square pan. Let rise. Cover with halved pitted plums or other fresh fruit, or any well drained canned fruit. Cover with "ruebel" crumbs: Mix with spoon: ½ cup flour, ½ cup sugar, 2 or 3 tablespoons melted shortening or salad oil.

Krimmsche Schnittchen *(Crimean slices)*

1 package yeast dissolved in
   ½ cup water plus 1
   teaspoon sugar
1 pound margarine (½ butter
   may be used)
1 teaspoon salt
4 tablespoons sugar
¾ cup milk (not heated)
3 eggs
6 cups flour

Nut topping
½ cup ground nuts
½ cup sugar
2 teaspoons cinnamon

Beat eggs well with sugar and salt, then add yeast mixture, milk, flour and margarine by hand. Place in refrigerator overnight. Next day roll out to ¼ inch thickness. Brush with an egg yolk mixed with about 2 tablespoons milk, then spread with nut topping. Let rise a bit and bake at 400° until golden brown (watch that they do not get dark).

Can be served as a tea cake.

Schnittchen *(or fruit rolls)*

2 cups flour
3 teaspoons baking powder
1 teaspoon salt
4 tablespoons shortening
⅔ cup milk

Sift dry ingredients and cut in shortening. Make a well and add milk, mixing well with a fork. Knead lightly on lightly floured board. Roll out to ¼ inch, fold on edge of dough to a 1 inch strip. Cut this double strip length of dough. Cut strip into 2 inch lengths. Repeat with remaining dough. Bake at 400° for 15 minutes or until golden brown.

Fruit Rolls: Roll out dough and place thick preserves or jam in a long line at least 1 inch from edge. Roll dough over to cover fruit. Seal along edge with a little milk or egg yolk. Repeat until dough is used up. Place on greased baking sheet and brush rolls with milk or egg yolk. Bake same as schnittchen. Cut in diagonal pieces when cool.

Traditional Classics—
Recipes and Menus

The Plain People

There are a number of Mennonites whose faith calls them to forsake modern dress and conveniences in order to live a godly, simple life. Depending on the group of which they are a part, this may include the use of horse and buggy for transportation. living without electricity or telephones and various dress codes.

Their recipes are those using products they produce on the farm. Foods are cooked and baked in their wood stoves. At mealtime there is always a hot oven.

Few homes have refrigeration or freezers. So the summer is busy with gardening, canning and drying. Some of these recipes are shared in this book.

Of special interest to you will be the menus they use for quiltings, barn raisings, funerals and weddings. Be sure to read the recipe for "Poached Eggs" (page 182)! It's a delightful surprise.

To learn more about the Mennonite and Amish faith and culture, write Good Books, Main Street, Intercourse, PA 17534 for a book catalog.

Quilting Bees

Quilting Bees are a common activity among many Mennonite women. The quilts are made for a family member's wedding gifts or some charitable benefit such as the relief sales.

Making a quilt is a time-consuming task. A quilt pattern is selected and fabric selected to cut into pieces that will make up the quilted top. After stitching these small pieces together, the assembled top, along with the soft fiber batting and fabric backing are pinned into a large quilt frame—ready for skilled hands to quilt into a single piece.

The quilting bee holds true to the saying "many hands make light work" as well as proving to be an enjoyable social time of talk and fellowship.

Here are several examples of the food that will be served by the hostess.

Quilting Dinner

mashed potatoes, buttered corn and lima beans, farmers pork sausage, coleslaw, company best pickles, peaches, Jam Jams (recipe below), Tapioca Fluff (page 183), Dried Apple Cake (page 184)

Afternoon Refreshments for Quilting Ladies

grape drink (homemade)
Poached Eggs (page 182)
butterscotch popcorn

Jam Jams

1 cup brown sugar, 1 cup shortening, 6 tablespoons corn syrup, 1 teaspoon vanilla, 2 eggs, 1¾ teaspoons soda, flour to make a stiff dough

Roll out and cut with cookie cutter, bake and put together with apple butter or raspberry jam.

Try them!

Poached Eggs

On dessert plates put 2 slices of Molasses Graham Bread (this looks like toast—recipe below) and a pile of sweetened whipped cream. Now top with a canned peach half, round side up. If you are counting your calories just put slices of graham bread together with honey and serve with tea.

Molasses Graham Bread

¼ cup sugar, 2 cups flour, 1½ teaspoons soda, 1 teaspoon salt, 1 teaspoon baking powder, 1¾ cups graham flour, ⅓ cup shortening, 2 eggs beaten, 1¾ cups sour milk or buttermilk, ¾ cup molasses

Sift dry ingredients and cut shortening into them.
Blend eggs, milk and molasses, pour into dry mixture, stir just enough to blend together. Bake in 2 greased loaf pans at 350° for 40 minutes.

Wedding Dinner for 100

8 loaves of bread, 2 pounds butter, 3 roast pans scalloped potatoes, 150 pieces boneless dinner ham, 12 cans sliced pineapple to decorate ham, 3 quarts fruit relish, 10 orange jellied molds, unmolded on lettuce, 14 quarts peas and corn mixed, fruit salad, 3 batches Shortbreads (page 52), 1 double batch Strawberries (page 55), 6 dozen pink angel squares, wedding cake and coffee

Funeral Dinner for 200

13 crocks peeled potatoes, creamed, 50 pounds bologna, 50 pounds cheese, 3 boxes soda biscuits, 4 crocks sour red beets, 3 crocks raw cabbage pickle, 20 loaves of bread, 3 pounds butter, 12 cups honey, 9 crocks applesauce, 7 crocks prepared dried apples, 25 dozen plain buns, 4 batches oatmeal muffins, 2 jars instant coffee

This seems to be a large amount of food but what is left over is served again at supper to the closest relatives who have stayed and then divided amongst the kind neighbors who helped with the work.

Threshers' Dinner

bread, butter, preserves, mashed potatoes, baked home-cured ham, creamed dried corn, bean salad, pickled baby corn, plums, caramel pudding, large oatmeal cookies, hot mince pie and homemade ice cream, coffee

Yellow Bean Salad

1 quart yellow (or green) beans (not raw), ½ onion chopped, 2 chopped hard boiled eggs, salt and pepper to taste
Dressing: 1 teaspoon vinegar, 1 teaspoon sugar, ¾ cup sour cream

Threshers' Supper

creamed potatoes, summer sausage, bread, butter, honey, cheese, corn on the cob, tomatoes, lettuce, mustard greens, pears, butterscotch sponge, elderberry pie

Creamed Potatoes

Slice potatoes thinly, add salt and some water. Cook. Add rich cream and sprinkle with sweet marjoram or parsley.

Tapioca Fluff

Heat 6 cups milk, 6 tablespoons quick-cooking tapioca, 1 cup sugar, 4 egg yolks. When boiling cook and stir for 5 minutes, not longer. Then remove from heat and add 4 egg whites beaten stiff and sweetened with ½ cup white sugar. Stir together for 2 minutes, then pour into serving dishes. Serves 12.

Dried Apple Cake

2 cups dried apples, 2 cups molasses, 1 cup butter, 2 cups brown sugar, 1 cup sour milk, 2 eggs, 2 teaspoons soda, 4 cups flour, spices

Soak apples in water overnight, then drain and simmer 1 hour in molasses. Add the butter and cool. Now add the rest of the ingredients and bake in loaf pans.

Barn Raising Dinner for 250 Men

When a fire destroys a barn in Amish and Mennonite communities, church members from near and far donate time, money, materials and tools for the rebuilding. Plans are carefully made, enabling a crew of several hundred male volunteers to erect a large barn in a single day. The women volunteer food and time to prepare meals for the men. Although hard work, it is an enjoyable social event as well.
The following is a typical amount of food to feed the workers.

24 loaves of bread, 5 pounds butter, 21 crocks potatoes, boiled and riced; 4 large roasters, Gravy Beef (page 186), 8 crocks carrots, boiled and buttered; 3 crocks carrot and cucumber pickle, 45 large jars applesauce, 12 crocks sweet apple schnitz and prunes, 350 Amish doughnuts, 5 gallons maple syrup, 45 lemon drop pies

There is usually enough left over for all women and children, which may number anywhere from 50–90.

Homemade Bread *(with fast rising yeast)*

Prepare yeast as package says, use 2 packages. Take 2 large spoonfuls lard, add 1 or 2 handfuls salt, a little sugar, about 1 cup, mix, add your yeast and enough liquid for the right amount of bread. Mix flour with this to form a slush. Let stand 20 minutes, then work stiff. Let stand, then mold and let rise and bake. This gives 4 to 5 large loaves and 2 coffee cakes. This is typical of recipes in some of the cookbooks of Old Order Mennonites.

To remove blood from quilt caused by finger pricks, dampen a small wad of the bat with water and place it on the blood stain for a half hour. Usually it draws out on the wad.

Rolly Polly

Make one recipe of biscuit dough. Take half and roll out, spread with apple butter, roll up and place on baking sheet. Do likewise with other half. Bake. Cut in pieces and serve with warm milk.

Apple Butter

20 medium sized apples, 1 cup of sieved pumpkin or pears for thickener, 1½ quarts apple cider, 1½ pounds white sugar, 1 teaspoon ground cinnamon, 1 teaspoon ground allspice, 1 teaspoon ground cloves

Wash and cut the apples into small pieces. Remove stem and blossom. Cover with water and boil until soft and put through sieve to remove skins and seeds. Bring cider to boil and add apple and remaining ingredients. Cook and stir until right thickness for spreading. Store in covered crocks in cool place.

Noodles

6 eggs, 4 tablespoons cold water, ½ teaspoon salt, 4 cups all-purpose flour

Mix eggs, water and salt well, add flour and knead about 100 times. Roll thin and cut in strips of width desired. Allow to dry thoroughly and store in jars or plastic containers.

Life was simple in the 'old days'.
We didn't need a serviceman to keep
the kitchen operating.

Homemade Mincemeat

1 pail (3 gallons) ground cooked beef, 3 pails ground apples, 1 dozen ground oranges (peelings and all), 5 pounds brown sugar, 27 cups white sugar, 3 gallons apple juice, 3 quarts lemon juice, 1 gallon dandelion wine, 1 gallon strong baking molasses, 4 tablespoons salt, 2 packages raisins, 6 ounces cinnamon, 3 ounces cloves, 2 ounces nutmeg, 2 ounces ginger

This makes 1 washtub full and should make anywhere from 60–100 pies and maybe more.

Creamed Dried Corn

From your leftover "corn on the cobs" cut off the kernels, spread thinly on cookie sheets and dry in a 250° oven. Stir often. Leave door open slightly for steam to escape. When real hard and brown in color, remove from oven and store in a tight container for as long as you wish. To prepare for dinner for 4 take 2 cups dried corn, 3 cups boiling water, salt to taste. Boil until corn is soft, adding water as necessary. Make a paste of flour and water, add and boil until thick. Add ½ cup cream.

Gravy Beef (steak in gravy)

Cut raw beef roast into serving pieces, flavor to taste and roast until tender. Now set pan on top of stove and cover with water and stir in flour paste. Boil until thick.

Marriage is the chalice that
holds the wine of love.

Butterscotch Sponge

1 cup brown sugar, 2 tablespoons butter, caramelize this and add 3½ cups hot milk, 4 beaten egg yolks, 1 package clear gelatin dissolved in ¼ cup cold water

When mixture is cold add 4 beaten egg whites and pour into serving dish lined with buttered and sugared graham wafer crumbs.

Soda Cheese

4 gallons skim milk. Heat to 98°. Put in large cheesecloth bag and squeeze out whey till dry. Put through food chopper to grind. Put in a crock and add 2 eggs well beaten and 2 tablespoons soda dissolved in 1 cup hot water. Add 1 cup cold water, mix and let stand overnight. Next morning cook in a double boiler adding 3 cups water and ½ cup sweet cream and 1 teaspoon caraway.

Egg or Easter Cheese

2 quarts milk (2% passes)
4–6 eggs
1 teaspoon salt
1 pint buttermilk

Using a buttered kettle, heat milk on moderate heat. (It scorches easily.) When steaming hot add the mixture of beaten eggs, buttermilk and salt. Stir well. Continue heating, stirring occasionally. Reduce heat when curds start to form. When curds and whey are fully separated (2–3 minutes more) pour all through a cloth lined colander or bag. Drain for 2 hours. Refrigerate. Serve with lots of fresh maple syrup.

Summer Sausage

2 parts beef and one part pork, ground very fine. For every 8 pounds meat take 5½ ounces salt, 4 ounces sugar (some folks use brown, others white), 1 ounce pepper, 2 tablespoons saltpeter, a little garlic if desired. Mix all spices before putting into meat. Put in ~~factory~~ cotton bags with sausage stuffer. Smoke 1 week.

Pork Sausage

For 50 pounds meat—1 pound salt, 5 tablespoons pepper

Mix well and put in casings with sausage stuffer. ½ package casings for 75 pounds.

To Cure Ham

5 pounds salt, 2 pounds brown sugar, 2 ounces saltpeter for 100 pounds of meat.

Rub the meat once every three days with ⅓ of mixture. After the last rubbing let meat sit in a wooden tub for a week to 10 days before smoking.

How to Boil Soap

30 pounds soap grease—butcher scraps, 6 pounds caustic soda, 3 gallons soft water

Boil 3 hours. Add water from time to time till 5 to 6 gallons more have been added. Add 5 pints salt. Stir well and put out fire. If you want it scented add 2 ounces oil of citronella to 60 pounds.

Dandelion Wine

Pick dandelion flower heads enough to make a gallon pail full, slightly packed. Place in a granite kettle and pour over 1 gallon boiling water. Cover, let stand 12 days stirring every day. Strain off the liquid, add 3½ pounds of sugar and thinly sliced orange and lemon, a few small pieces of ginger root. Boil gently for 20 minutes. When lukewarm, lay a piece of toast on top with ¼ ounce of yeast spread on. Cover, let stand 2 days. Strain, put in gallon glass jug with a cork stopper. Leave for 6 months or longer. You may have to watch that stopper, he'll fly off, just put back on again.

Dried Apples

Peel and core Tolman Sweet apples and slice apples in eighths. Heat in oven at 200° stirring often. Leave oven door open to let steam escape. Will take 24 hours. Store in jars not necessarily airtight. Before cooking soak overnight in cold water. Good with prunes or raisins. If you want something special add an orange, rind and all, which you have put through the meat chopper. Add sugar.

Potato Soup

Dice several potatoes, add a little onion and salt. Boil until soft. Add whole milk and heat. Put a piece of butter in a frying pan and melt. Cut a slice or two of bread cut in cubes and brown in butter. Add to soup, also a sprinkle of pepper. This soup was served every Monday night if there were leftover raw potatoes that had been peeled for Sunday.

Grandma's Remedies

Bread and Milk Poultices

Heat milk in a pan. Put in a slice of white bread and leave until milk has soaked up and bread is quite warm.

Place on infected sores or boils; keep the treatment up for at least an hour using 2 or more pieces of bread and applying them directly to sore keeping them as warm as the patient can stand it. This is highly recommended to bring boils to a head.

Simple Ointment

2 ounces sulfur
½ pound melted lard

Mix thoroughly and allow to harden. Good for piles, itch and skin diseases in general.

Homemade Liniment

1 pint pure cider vinegar
3 eggs
3 ounces turpentine
3 ounces spirits of camphor

Beat eggs in a deep bowl 10 minutes. Add slowly, first turpentine, then vinegar and last the camphor, stirring all the time. Shake 2 or 3 times a day for 2 days. Then it is ready to use.

Old Fashioned Cough Remedy

Boil one lemon slowly for 10 minutes. This softens the lemon so more juice will be gotten out of it. Cut the lemon in two and extract the juice with a squeezer. Put the juice into an ordinary drinking glass. Add 2 tablespoons of glycerine. Stir well, then fill up the glass with honey. Stir with a spoon before taking.
Dosage: 1 teaspoon when you have a coughing spell. If cough is severe take 1 teaspoon every 3 hours.

Claims for Honey

1. If you are rundown, irritable and always tired, try taking 3 or 4 teaspoons honey a day for several months. It is good for insomnia, constipation, and poor blood.
2. If you scald or burn yourself, apply honey immediately. It will heal rapidly.
3. Twitching of the eyelids or the corner of the mouth can be cured by taking 2 teaspoons honey each meal.
4. Muscle cramps can be cured by taking 2 teaspoons of honey at each meal.

Teas and What They Are Good For

All teas are made the same way:
¼ cup of dried leaves or roots
2 cups boiling water
a little honey

Camomile flowers	diarrhea
Bone set	sick with a cold and fever
Thistle root	for rheumatism
Mullet leaves	anemia
Burdock tea	kidneys and bladder
Black strap molasses	arthritis
Sage tea	stomach settler

Mustard Plaster

1 tablespoon mustard
4 tablespoons flour
water to moisten

Spread on clean white cotton. Place plaster over patient's lungs which have been thoroughly covered with petroleum jelly or other grease. Watch *very closely*. Remove when skin is a rosy pink. A mustard plaster will burn.

Hair Tonic

Losing your hair? Try this:
1 pint sage tea, using ½ cup sage leaves pressed down
1 ounce glycerine
2 ounces bay rum
Mix all together and apply daily.

Cider Vinegar

Claims for cider vinegar have been sent in as a reliable cure for almost anything. Here are a few:

Impetigo:
Cider vinegar just as it comes from the bottle applied to infected part of skin 6 times a day. This treatment also good for ringworm and shingles.

Poison Ivy:
Use equal parts of cider vinegar and water. Apply to affected part and allow to dry. Do this often.

Sore throat? Gargle with cider vinegar.

Lily Whiskey

Fill a jar with the petals of the Madonna Lily. Get a bottle of real good whiskey. Fill the jar so the petals are all covered, as they settle down, add more whiskey. This is especially good for burns and sores.

Apply the petals to infected sores!

Directory of Mennonite Relief Sales —United States

Here is a listing of all current Relief Sales.
For further information contact:

Mennonite Central Committee
704 Main St.
Box 500
Akron, PA 17501

State	City	Date
California	Fresno	First Saturday of April
Colorado	Rocky Ford	Third Saturday of October
Illinois	Arthur	Fourth Saturday of August
Illinois	Peoria	Third Friday and Saturday of March
Indiana	Goshen	Fourth Weekend of September
Indiana	Montgomery	Second Saturday of July
Iowa	Iowa City	Memorial Day Weekend
Kansas	Hutchinson	Second Saturday of April, (unless Easter Weekend, then First)
Michigan	Fairview	First Saturday of August
Missouri	Harrisonville	Second Saturday in October
Nebraska	Aurora	First Saturday of April, (Unless Easter Weekend, then Second)

State	City	Date
North Dakota	Minot	First Saturday of April
Ohio	Kidron	First Saturday of August
Oklahoma	Fairview	Always the Friday and Saturday after Thanksgiving
Oregon	Albany	Second Saturday in October
Pennsylvania	Gap	Second Saturday of August
Pennsylvania	Harrisburg	First Saturday of April, (Unless Easter Weekend, then Second) A very large sale!
Pennsylvania	Johnstown	Fourth Thursday, Friday and Saturday of October
Pennsylvania	Lancaster	Second Thursday of March Selling livestock and hay
New York	Bath	Last Saturday in July
South Dakota	Sioux Falls	Fourth Friday of August
Texas	Houston	First Saturday of November
Virginia	Fisherville	Last Saturday of September
Washington	Ritzville	First Saturday in October
Wisconsin	Jefferson	Second Saturday of August

Directory of Mennonite Relief Sales — Canada

State	City	Date
Alberta	Tofield/Coaldale	July 17-18 Weekend
British Columbia	Black Creek	
British Columbia	Clearbroo	September 19 Weekend
British Columbia	Kelowna	September 26 Weekend
British Columbia	Prince George	October 3 Weekend
Ontario	Black Creek	September 19 Weekend
Ontario	Guelph	February 20 Weekend Sells mostly cattle
Ontario	New Hamburg	May 30 Weekend A very large sale!
Manitoba	Brandon	August15 Weekend
Manitoba	Morris	September 19 Weekend
Saskatchewan	Hague	June 13 Weekend' Sells mostly grain and farm supplies
Saskatchewan	Saskatoon	May 29-30 Weekend

For further information, you can write to the provincial MCC
Headquarters listed below:

MCC Ontario
50 Kent Ave.
Kitchener, Ont. N2G 3R1

MCC British Columbia
31872 S. Fraser Way
Box 2038
Clearbrook BC V2T 3TB

MC Saskatchewan
600 45th Street West
Saskatoon, Sask. S7L 5W9

MCC Alberta
76 Skyline Crescent NE
Calgary, Alta. T2K 5X7

MCC Manitoba
134 Plaza Drive
Winnipeg, Man. R3T 5K9

Recipe Index

Almonds	Almond Torte	32
Almonds	Almond Shortbread	52
Apple Butter	Apple Butter Pudding	107
Apple Butter	Rolly Polly	184
Apple butter	Apple Butter Pie	120
Apples	Apple Strudel	98
Apples	Apple Fritters	20
Apples	Apple Pancakes	22
Apples	Apple Squares	57
Apples	Apple Delight	100
Apples	Apple Salad	101
Apples	Apple Pudding	101
Apples	Apple Dumplings	102
Apples	Apple Bars	106
Apples	Luscious Apple Pie	115
Apples	Dutch Apple Pie	116
Apples	Green Tomato Mincemeat	121
Apples	Mincemeat	121
Apples	Fruit and Tomato Relish	127
Apples	Spiced Crab Apples	132
Apples	Cranberry Salad	148
Apples	Schmoor Kohl	168
Apples	Apple Moos	169
Apples	Apple Strudel	170
Apples	Dried Apple Cake	184
Apples	Apple Butter	185
Apples	Homemade Mincemeat	185
Apples	Dried Apples	188
Applesauce	Applesauce Nut Bread	11
Applesauce	Grandmother Cressman's Applesauce Cake	32
Applesauce	Dorda Pie	119
Bacon	Pork and Beans	79
Bananas	Banana Nut Bread	12
Bananas	Banana Muffins	17
Bananas	Banana Cake	26
Bananas	Orange Banana Salad	149
Bananas	Lemon-Line Gelatin Salad	150
Bananas	Far East Fruit Plate	155
Beans	Pork and Beans	79
Beans	Mustard Bean Pickles	131
Beans	Canned Bean Salad	145
Beans	Mexicali Salad Ring	153
Beans	Cream of Bean Soup	161
Beans	Yellow Bean Salad	183
Beef, Ground	Beef Macaroni Dinner	71
Beef, Hamburger	Chow Mein	71
Beef, Hamburger	A Quickie	72
Beef, Hamburger	Porcupines	73
Beef, Ground	Bar-B-Que Burgers	73
Beef, Hamburger	Lasagna	74

Beef, Ground	Cabbage Rolls	77
Beef	Sweet and Sour Meatballs	85
Beef	Hamburger Roll-Ups	86
Beef	Beef Stroganoff	87
Beef	Beef Oriental	88
Beef, Hamburger	Ribbon Meat Loaf	88
Beef, Hamburger	Juicy Meat Loaf	89
Beef	Steak Rouladin	90
Beef	Mincemeat	121
Beef, Hamburger	Hamburger Soup	162
Beef	Borscht	167
Beef	Piramanie	167
Beef	Fleisch Piroschky	168
Beef	Homemade Mincemeat	185
Beef	Gravy Beef	186
Beef	Summer Sausage	187
Beets	Fresh Red Beets as a Vegetable	80
Beets	Mother's Favorite Pickle	127
Beets	Pickled Beets	131
Beets	Horseradish Salad	154
Blueberries	Blueberry Fruit Pies	114
Bran	Moist Date Bran Loaf	15
Bran	Bran Muffins	16
Bread	Bread Dressing	92
Butterscotch Chips	Rocky Road Squares	58
Cabbage	Cabbage Rolls	77
Cabbage	Hot Cabbage	80
Cabbage	Sweet and Sour Cabbage	80
Cabbage	Mother's Favorite Pickle	127
Cabbage	Cabbage Salad	146
Cabbage	2 Week Cole Slaw	147
Cabbage	Coleslaw Parfait Salad	152
Cabbage	Schmoor Kohl	168
Cakes and Frostings	Lazy Daisy Oatmeal Cake	25
Cakes and Frostings	Queen Elizabeth Cake	25
Cakes and Frostings	Banana Cake	26
Cakes and Frostings	Maple-Nut Chiffon Cake	26
Cakes and Frostings	Two-Egg Chiffon Cake	27
Cakes and Frostings	Easy Icing	27
Cakes and Frostings	Sour Cream Spice Cake	27
Cakes and Frostings	Black Chocolate Cake	28
Cakes and Frostings	Mocha Icing	28
Cakes and Frostings	Fruit Cocktail Cake	28
Cakes and Frostings	Marble Chiffon Cake	29
Cakes and Frostings	Grandma's Cocoa Cake	30
Cakes and Frostings	Graham Wafer Cake	30
Cakes and Frostings	Wacky Cake	31
Cakes and Frostings	Sauerkraut Cake	31
Cakes and Frostings	Grandmother Cressman's Applesauce Cake	32
Cakes and Frostings	Almond Torte	32
Cakes and Frostings	Icing	33
Cakes and Frostings	Sauce for Angel Food Cake	33
Cakes and Frostings	Chocolate Icing	33

Cakes and Frostings	Maple Cream Icing	33
Cakes and Frostings	Black Forest Torte	34
Cakes and Frostings	Christmas Cake	34
Cakes and Frostings	Fruit Cake	35
Cakes and Frostings	Christmas Cake	35
Cakes and Frostings	Nusskuchen	171
Cakes and Frostings	Hungarian Cheesecake	172
Cakes and Frostings	Dried Apple Cake	184
Candies	Very Old Fudge	39
Candies	Horehound Candy	39
Candies	Chocolate Nut Caramels	39
Candies	Maple Cream Candy	39
Candies	Peanut Butter Fudge	40
Candies	Cracker-Jack	40
Candies	Candied Grapefruit	40
Candies	Children's Favorite Maple Cream	40
Candies	Caramel Corn	41
Candies	Peanut Brittle	41
Candies	Chocolate Fudge	41
Candies	Easy Caramels	42
Candies	Divinity Fudge	42
Candies	Orange Candy	42
Canned Tomatoes	Hamburger Tomato Casserole	72
Caramels	Caramel Krisp	60
Carrots	Carrot Bread	12
Carrots	Carrot Potato Chowder	80
Carrots	Steamed Carrot Pudding	108
Carrots	Marinated Carrot Salad	154
Casseroles and Supper Dishes	Delicious Chicken Casserole	69
Casseroles and Supper Dishes	Chicken with Rice Casserole	69
Casseroles and Supper Dishes	Tuna Noodle Casserole	69
Casseroles and Supper Dishes	Tuna Casserole	70
Casseroles and Supper Dishes	Turkey Pie with English Pastry	70
Casseroles and Supper Dishes	English Pastry	70
Casseroles and Supper Dishes	Beef-Macaroni Dinner	71
Casseroles and Supper Dishes	Chow Mein	71
Casseroles and Supper Dishes	A Quickie	72
Casseroles and Supper Dishes	Seven Layer Dinner	72
Casseroles and Supper Dishes	Hamburger Tomato Casserole	72
Casseroles and Supper Dishes	Porcupines	73
Casseroles and Supper Dishes	Sauerkraut and Pork	73
Casseroles and Supper Dishes	Bar-B-Que Burgers	73
Casseroles and Supper Dishes	Lasagna	74
Casseroles and Supper Dishes	Wiener Casserole	74
Casseroles and Supper Dishes	Spinach Pie	75
Casseroles and Supper Dishes	Frankfurter Cheese Boats	75
Casseroles and Supper Dishes	Big Catch Casserole	75
Casseroles and Supper Dishes	Corn Casserole	76
Casseroles and Supper Dishes	Super Eggs on Toast	76
Casseroles and Supper Dishes	Pickled Chicken Gizzards	76
Casseroles and Supper Dishes	Salmon Patties	77
Casseroles and Supper Dishes	Cabbage Rolls	77
Casseroles and Supper Dishes	Cheese Soufflé	78
Casseroles and Supper Dishes	Cheese and Bread Casserole	78

Casseroles and Supper Dishes	Sweet and Sour Pigtails or Spareribs	78
Casseroles and Supper Dishes	Piggy Casserole	79
Casseroles and Supper Dishes	Baked Beans	79
Casseroles and Supper Dishes	Pork and Beans	79
Casseroles and Supper Dishes	Fresh Red Beets as a Vegetable	80
Casseroles and Supper Dishes	Hot Cabbage	80
Casseroles and Supper Dishes	Sweet and Sour Cabbage	80
Casseroles and Supper Dishes	Carrot Potato Chowder	80
Casseroles and Supper Dishes	Party Sandwich Loaf	81
Casseroles and Supper Dishes	Party Buns	81
Casseroles and Supper Dishes	Kielke	167
Casseroles and Supper Dishes	Piramanie	167
Casseroles and Supper Dishes	Fleisch Piroschky	167
Casseroles and Supper Dishes	Bubbat	169
Casseroles and Supper Dishes	Glums Vareneki	169
Casseroles and Supper Dishes	Zwetschen Knoedel	170
Casseroles and Supper Dishes	Creamed Potatoes	183
Casseroles and Supper Dishes	Creamed Dried Corn	186
Cauliflower	Cucumber Relish	129
Celery	Green Hot Dog Relish	132
Celery	Festive Party Salad	150
Cheese	Soda Cheese	186
Cheese	Egg or Easter Cheese	187
Cherries	Cherry Tea Bread	13
Cherries	Cherry Surprises	54
Cherries	Charming Cherry Bars	58
Cherries	"O Henry" Squares	59
Cherries	Cherry Dumplings	102
Cherries	Cherry Fruit Pies	114
Cherry Pie Filling	Black Forest Torte	34
Chicken	Delicious Chicken Casserole	69
Chicken	Chicken with Rice Casserole	69
Chicken	Party Buns	81
Chicken	Sweet and Sour Chicken Wings	85
Chicken	Leftover Chicken Croquettes	87
Chicken	Stewed Chicken Dinner with Biscuits	92
Chicken	Chicken Pot Pie	94
Chicken	Chicken Salad	153
Chicken	Chicken Soup	163
Chicken	Chicken Noodle Soup	163
Chicken Gizzards	Pickled Chicken Gizzards	76
Cinnamon	Cinnamon Rolls	5
Coconut	Fruit Cocktail Cake	28
Coconut	Graham Wafer Cake	30
Coconut	Fruit Cake	35
Coconut	Butter Crunch Cookies	48
Coconut	Tempters	51
Coconut	Coconut Kisses	52
Coconut	Chocolate Swirls	53
Coconut	Coconut Clusters	54
Coconut	Strawberry Cookies	55

Coconut	Raspberry Squares	59
Coconut	Tropical Bars	61
Coconut	Butter Nut Chews	61
Coconut	Magic Cookie Bars	62
Coconut	Coconut Pie	122
Coffee Cakes	(See Quick Breads)	
Cookies, Squares and Bar Cookies	Oatmeal Raisin Cookies	45
Cookies, Squares and Bar Cookies	Rice Flake Balls	45
Cookies, Squares and Bar Cookies	Melting Moments	45
Cookies, Squares and Bar Cookies	Rolled Oatmeal Cookies	46
Cookies, Squares and Bar Cookies	Molasses Krinkles	46
Cookies, Squares and Bar Cookies	Sugar Cookies	47
Cookies, Squares and Bar Cookies	Oatmeal Cereal Cookies	47
Cookies, Squares and Bar Cookies	Butter Crunch Cookies	48
Cookies, Squares and Bar Cookies	Cherry Winks	48
Cookies, Squares and Bar Cookies	Oatmeal-Walnut Cookies	49
Cookies, Squares and Bar Cookies	Quickest Easiest Oatmeal Cookies	49
Cookies, Squares and Bar Cookies	Peppermint Cookies with Milk	50
Cookies, Squares and Bar Cookies	Unbaked Chocolate Roll	50
Cookies, Squares and Bar Cookies	Cornflake Drops	50
Cookies, Squares and Bar Cookies	Marmalade Nut Cookies	51
Cookies, Squares and Bar Cookies	Tempters	51
Cookies, Squares and Bar Cookies	Cornflake Macaroons	51
Cookies, Squares and Bar Cookies	Walnut Logs	52
Cookies, Squares and Bar Cookies	Shortbreads	52
Cookies, Squares and Bar Cookies	Coconut Kisses	52
Cookies, Squares and Bar Cookies	Health Cookies	53
Cookies, Squares and Bar Cookies	Fruit Jumbos	53
Cookies, Squares and Bar Cookies	Chocolate Swirls	53
Cookies, Squares and Bar Cookies	Cherry Surprises	54
Cookies, Squares and Bar Cookies	Coconut or Chocolate Clusters	54
Cookies, Squares and Bar Cookies	Brownies	54
Cookies, Squares and Bar Cookies	Apple Blossom Cookies	55
Cookies, Squares and Bar Cookies	Strawberry Cookies	55
Cookies, Squares and Bar Cookies	Mint Chocolate Sticks	56
Cookies, Squares and Bar Cookies	Pecan Fingers	56
Cookies, Squares and Bar Cookies	Chocolate Marshmallow Squares	56
Cookies, Squares and Bar Cookies	Apple Squares	57
Cookies, Squares and Bar Cookies	Custard Cream Bars	57
Cookies, Squares and Bar Cookies	Charming Cherry Bars	58
Cookies, Squares and Bar Cookies	Rocky Road Squares	58
Cookies, Squares and Bar Cookies	Raspberry Squares	59
Cookies, Squares and Bar Cookies	"O Henry" Squares	59
Cookies, Squares and Bar Cookies	Fruit Squares	60
Cookies, Squares and Bar Cookies	Marshmallow Delights	60
Cookies, Squares and Bar Cookies	Caramel Krisp	60
Cookies, Squares and Bar Cookies	Tropical Bars	61
Cookies, Squares and Bar Cookies	Butter Nut Chews	61
Cookies, Squares and Bar Cookies	Oatmeal Squares	62
Cookies, Squares and Bar Cookies	Graham Wafer Squares	62
Cookies, Squares and Bar Cookies	Magic Cookie Bars	62
Cookies, Squares and Bar Cookies	Old Fashioned Raisin Bars	63
Cookies, Squares and Bar Cookies	Lemon Squares	63
Cookies, Squares and Bar Cookies	Date Pinwheels	64

Cookies, Squares, or Bar Cookies	Christmas Cookies	171
Cookies, Squares, and Bar Cookies	Jam Jams	181
Corn	Creamed Dried Corn	119
Corn	Corn Casserole	76
Corn	Pickled Baby Corn	133
Corn	Creamed Dried Corn	186
Corn Flakes	Butter Crunch Cookies	48
Cornflakes	Cornflake Drops	50
Cornflakes	Cornflake Macaroons	51
Cornflakes	Caramel Krisp	60
Cottage Cheese	Vegetable Salad	151
Cottage Cheese	Fruited Cheese Salad	153
Cottage Cheese	Far East Fruit Plate	155
Cottage Cheese	Glums Vareneki	169
Cottage Cheese	Hungarian Cheesecake	172
Cottage cheese	Cheese Spread for Paska	174
Cranberries	Cranberry Punch	141
Cranberries	Cranberry Salad	148
Cranberry Sauce	Cranberry-Raspberry Salad	151
Cream Cheese	Cheese Cake	97
Cream Cheese	Festive Party Salad	150
Cream Cheese	Cream Cheese Salad	152
Crushed Pineapple	Tropical Bars	61
Cucumbers	Copper Pickles	128
Cucumbers	Company Best Pickles	129
Cucumbers	Cucumber Relish	129
Cucumbers	Queen of Pickles	130
Cucumbers	Sweet Pickles Sticks	130
Cucumbers	Green Hot Dog Relish	132
Cucumbers	Dill Pickles	133
Currants	Mincemeat	121
Currants	Black Currant Preserves	134
Currants	Black Currant Drink	137
Currants	Black Currant Lemonade	137
Dandelions	Dandelion Drink	141
Dandelions	Dandelion Wine	188
Dates	Moist Date Bran Loaf	15
Dates	Date Nut Muffins	16
Dates	Queen Elizabeth Cake	25
Dates	Rice Flake Balls	45
Dates	Rolled Oatmeal Cookies	46
Dates	Cherry Winks	48
Dates	Fruit Jumbos	53
Dates	Date Pinwheels	64
Dates	Date Oatmeal Squares	65
Desserts	Cheesecake	97
Desserts	Cut Glass Cake	97
Desserts	Mandarin Orange Delight	98
Desserts	Bavarian Cream	98
Desserts	Orange Delight Dessert	99
Desserts	Seven Cents Pudding	99
Desserts	24 Hour Salad	100
Desserts	Apple Delight	100
Desserts	Apple Salad	101
Desserts	Apple Pudding	101

Desserts	Foamy Rum Sauce	101
Desserts	Dumplings-Lemon, Apple, Cherry, Maple	102
Desserts	Apple Dumplings	102
Desserts	Caramel Pudding	103
Desserts	Prune Pudding	103
Desserts	Frozen Berry Fluff	103
Desserts	Lemon Fluff Dessert	104
Desserts	Rhubarb Tarte	104
Desserts	Rhubarb Cake Pudding	105
Desserts	Raspberry Dessert	105
Desserts	Rice Fluff	106
Desserts	Apple Bars	106
Desserts	Spicy Fudge Pudding	107
Desserts	Apple Butter Pudding	107
Desserts	Dump Cake	108
Desserts	Steamed Carrot Cake	108
Desserts	Home-Made Ice Cream	109
Desserts	Home-Made Ice Cream	109
Desserts	Apple Moos	169
Desserts	Apple Strudel	170
Desserts	Fastnacht Doughnuts	172
Desserts	Rollkuchen	173
Desserts	Piroschky	173
Desserts	Raised Piroschky	176
Desserts	Krimmsche Schnittchen	177
Desserts	Schnittchen	177
Desserts	"Poached Eggs"	182
Desserts	Tapioca Fluff	183
Desserts	Rolly Polly	184
Desserts	Butterscotch Sponge	186
Desserts	Dried Apples	188
Doughnuts	(See Quick Breads)	
Dried Apricots	Apricot Brazil Bread	11
Elderberries	Elderberry Fruit Pies	114
Elderberries	Sour Cream Elderberry Pie	118
Fish	Baked Fish en Papillote	93
Fritters	(See Quick Breads)	
Fruit Preserves	Schnittchen	177
Gooseberries	Gooseberry Pie Filling	119
Gooseberries	Gooseberry Catsup	131
Graham Wafer Crumbs	Graham Wafer Cake	30
Graham Wafer Crumbs	Unbaked Chocolate Roll	50
Graham Wafer Crumbs	Custard Cream Bars	57
Grapes	Grape Pie	116
Grapes	Grape Juice	137
Ham	Baked Ham	86
Hamburger	Hamburger Tomato Casserole	72
Heart	Pickled Heart	89
Honey	Dutch Honey Bread	13
Jams/Marmalades	(See Pickles and Relishes)	
Lemons	Lemon Tea Bread	14
Lemons	Lemon Squares	63
Lemons	Lemon Dumplings	102

Lemons	Lemon Sponge Pie	117
Lemons	Montgomery Count or	
	Lemon Drop Pie	120
Lemons	Lemon-Orange Concentrate	141
Liver	Baked Liver	93
Main Dishes	Beef Stroganoff	9
Main Dishes	Sweet and Sour Chicken Wings	85
Main Dishes	Sweet and Sour Meatballs	85
Main Dishes	Hamburger Roll-Ups	86
Main Dishes	Sauce for Roll-Ups	86
Main Dishes	Baked Ham	86
Main Dishes	Barbecued Spareribs	87
Main Dishes	Leftover Turkey or	
	Chicken Croquettes	87
Main Dishes	Beef Stroganoff	87
Main Dishes	Beef Oriental	88
Main Dishes	Ribbon Meat Loaf	88
Main Dishes	Juicy Meat Loaf	89
Main Dishes	Pickled Heart and Tongue	89
Main Dishes	Steak Rouladin	90
Main Dishes	Spanish Veal	90
Main Dishes	Pork Chops	91
Main Dishes	Pork Chops and Rice Colonial	91
Main Dishes	Tea Biscuits Supreme	91
Main Dishes	Stewed Chicken Dinner	
	with Biscuits	92
Main Dishes	Bread Dressing	92
Main Dishes	Easy Dressing for Turkey	92
Main Dishes	Baked Liver	93
Main Dishes	Baked Fish en Papillote	93
Main Dishes	Chicken Pot Pie	94
Main Dishes	Dough for Pot Pie	94
Main Dishes	Gravy Beef	186
Main Dishes	Summer Sausage	187
Main Dishes	Pork Sausage	187
Maple Syrup	Maple Dumplings	102
Maple Syrup	Maple Walnut Pie	116
Maple Syrup	Shoofly Pie	117
Maple Syrup	Vanilla Pie	118
Marmalade	Marmalade Nut Cookies	51
Meat Curing	How To Cure Ham	187
Menus	Quilting Dinner	181
Menus	Afternoon Refreshments	
	for Quilting Ladies	181
Menus	Wedding Dinner for 100	182
Menus	Funeral Dinner for 200	182
Menus	Threshers' Dinner	183
Menus	Threshers' Supper	183
Menus	Barn Raising Dinner	
	for 250 Men	184
Mincemeat	Mincemeat Tea Bread	14
Miscellaneous.	Apple Butter	185
Miscellaneous.	Noodles	185
Muffins	(See Quick Breads)	

Oatmeal	Rolled Oat Bread	4
Oatmeal	Oatmeal Rolls	7
Oatmeal	Oatmeal Muffins	17
Oatmeal	Lazy Daisy Oatmeal Cake	25
Oatmeal	Oatmeal Raisin Cookies	45
Oatmeal	Rolled Oatmeal Cookies	46
Oatmeal	Oatmeal Cereal Cookies	47
Oatmeal	Quickest Easiest	
	Oatmeal Cookies	49
Oatmeal	Oatmeal Shortbreads	52
Oatmeal	Health Cookies	53
Oatmeal	Oatmeal Squares	62
Oatmeal	Date Oatmeal Squares	65
Onions	Fruit and Tomato Relish	127
Onions	Copper Pickles	128
Onions	Cucumber Relish	129
Onions	Green Hot Dog Relish	132
Onions	Tomato Juice	138
Onions	Wiener Potato Soup	161
Orange	Lemon-Orange Concentrate	141
Orange Rind	Orange Candy	42
Oranges	Peach Conserve	134
Oranges	Fruited Cheese Salad	153
Oranges	Mexicali Salad Ring	153
Oranges	Far East Fruit Plate	155
Oysters	Oyster Soup	164
Pancakes	(See Quick Breads)	
Pastries	(See Pies and Tarts)	113
Peaches	Peach Fruit Pies	114
Peaches	Winter Peach Pie	117
Peaches	Peach Conserve	134
Peaches	"Poached Eggs"	182
Peanut Butter	Peanut Butter Fudge	40
Peanuts	Peanut Brittle	41
Pears	Fruit and Tomato Relish	127
Pecans	Cherry Winks	48
Pecans	Pecan Fingers	56
Pecans	Butter Nut Chews	61
Pecans	Maple Walnut or Pecan Pie	116
Peppers	Queen of Pickles	130
Peppers	Queen of Pickles	130
Peppers	Green Hot Dog Relish	132
Peppers	Green Hot Dog Relish	132
Pickles and Relishes	Mother's Favorite Pickle	127
Pickles and Relishes	Fruit and Tomato Relish	127
Pickles and Relishes	Tomato Butter	127
Pickles and Relishes	Pickled Watermelon Rind	128
Pickles and Relishes	Pickled Eggs	128
Pickles and Relishes	Copper Pickles	128
Pickles and Relishes	Company Best Pickles	129
Pickles and Relishes	Cucumber Relish	129
Pickles and Relishes	Queen of Pickles	130
Pickles and Relishes	Sweet Pickle Sticks	130
Pickles and Relishes	Mustard Bean Pickles	131

Pickles and Relishes	Pickled Beets	131
Pickles and Relishes	Gooseberry Catsup	131
Pickles and Relishes	Green Hot Dog Relish	132
Pickles and Relishes	Spiced Crab Apples	132
Pickles and Relishes	Pickled Baby Corn	133
Pickles and Relishes	Dill Pickles	133
Pickles and Relishes	Heavenly Jam	133
Pickles and Relishes	Tomato Marmalade	133
Pickles and Relishes	Strawberry Rhubarb Jam	134
Pickles and Relishes	Peach Conserve	134
Pickles and Relishes	Black Currant Preserves	134
Pickles and Relishes	Black Currant	134
Pies and Tarts	Dutch Apple Pie	116
Pies and Tarts	Fruit Pies	114
Pies and Tarts	Luscious Apple Pie	115
Pies and Tarts	Maple Walnut or Pecan Pie	116
Pies and Tarts	Pastries	113
Pies and Tarts	Pumpkin Pie	43
Pies and Tarts	Relief Sale Strawberry Pie	115
Pies and Tarts	Rhubarb Pie with Meringue	115
Pies and Tarts	Strawberry Pie	114
Pies and Tarts	Grape Pie	116
Pies and Tarts	Winter Peach Pie	117
Pies and Tarts	Lemon Sponge Pie	117
Pies and Tarts	Shoofly Pie	117
Pies and Tarts	Vanilla Pie	118
Pies and Tarts	Easy Pumpkin Pie	118
Pies and Tarts	Sour Cream Elderberry Pie	118
Pies and Tarts	Rhubarb Strawberry Pie	118
Pies and Tarts	Dorda Pie	119
Pies and Tarts	Gooseberry Pie Filling	119
Pies and Tarts	Raisin Cream Pie	119
Pies and Tarts	Montgomery County or Lemon Drop Pie	120
Pies and Tarts	Apple Butter Pie	120
Pies and Tarts	Grasshopper Pie	120
Pies and Tarts	Green Tomato Mincemeat	121
Pies and Tarts	Mincemeat	121
Pies and Tarts	Pineapple Bavarian Pie	122
Pies and Tarts	Coconut Pie	122
Pies and Tarts	Buttermilk Pie	123
Pies and Tarts	Butter Tarts	123
Pies and Tarts	Homemade Mincemeat	185
Pineapple	Dump Cake	108
Pineapple	Pineapple Bavarian Pie	122
Pineapple	Lemon-Line Gelatin Salad	150
Pineapple	Cream Cheese Salad	152
Pineapple	Chicken Salad	153
Pineapple	Far East Fruit Plate	155
Pineapple	Hungarian Cheesecake	172
Plums	Zwetschen Knoedel	170
Popped Corn	Caramel Corn	41
Pork	Seven Layer Dinner	72
Pork	Sauerkraut and Pork	73

Pork, Pigtails	Sweet and Sour Pigtails	78
Pork	Sweet and Sour Spareribs	78
Pork, Ground	Piggy Casserole	79
Pork	Mincemeat	121
Pork	Smoked Sausage Potato Soup	162
Pork	Bubbat	169
Pork	Summer Sausage	187
Pork	Pork Sausage	187
Pork Chops	Pork Chops	91
Pork Chops	Pork Chops and Rice Colonial	91
Potatoes	Seven Layer Dinner	72
Potatoes	Wiener Casserole	74
Potatoes	Carrot Potato Chowder	80
Potatoes	Potato Salad	146
Potatoes	Hot Potato Salad	147
Potatoes	Wiener Potato Soup	161
Potatoes	Hamburger Soup	162
Potatoes	Smoked Sausage Potato Soup	162
Potatoes	Butter Soup	164
Potatoes	Borscht	167
Potatoes	Zwetschen Knoedel	170
Potatoes	Creamed Potatoes	183
Potatoes	Potato Soup	188
Prunes	Prune Pudding	103
Prunes	Schmoor Kohl	168
Pumpkin	Pumpkin Bread	15
Pumpkin	Easy Pumpkin Pie	118
Punches and Drinks	Black Currant Drink	137
Punches and Drinks	Blank Currant Lemonade	137
Punches and Drinks	Grape Juice	137
Punches and Drinks	Tomato Juice	138
Punches and Drinks	Eggnog	138
Punches and Drinks	Raspberry Vinegar	138
Punches and Drinks	Mint Tea	138
Punches and Drinks	Quantity Fruit Punch	139
Punches and Drinks	For the Punch Bowl	139
Punches and Drinks	Fruit Punch for 50	140
Punches and Drinks	Veranda Punch	140
Punches and Drinks	Friendship Tea	140
Punches and Drinks	For the Punch Bowl	140
Punches and Drinks	Lemon-Orange Concentrate	141
Punches and Drinks	Cranberry Punch	141
Punches and Drinks	Dandelion Drink	141
Punches and Drinks	Homemade Rhubarb Juice	142
Punches and Drinks	Dandelion Wine	188
Quick Breads	Apricot Brazil Bread	11
Quick Breads	Applesauce Nut Bread	11
Quick Breads	Banana Nut Bread	12
Quick Breads	Carrot Bread	12
Quick Breads	Cherry Tea Bread	13
Quick Breads	Dutch Honey Bread	13
Quick Breads	Lemon Tea Bread	14
Quick Breads	Mincemeat Tea Bread	14
Quick Breads	Pumpkin Bread	15

Quick Breads	Moist Date Bran Loaf	15
Quick Breads	Date Nut Muffins	16
Quick Breads	Bran Muffins	16
Quick Breads	Banana Muffins	17
Quick Breads	Oatmeal Muffins	17
Quick Breads	Tea Biscuits	17
Quick Breads	Easy Scones	18
Quick Breads	Johnny Cake I	18
Quick Breads	Johnny Cake II	18
Quick Breads	Doughnuts	18
Quick Breads	German Buns	19
Quick Breads	Relief Sale Doughnuts	19
Quick Breads	Relief Sale Teaballs	20
Quick Breads	Teaballs	20
Quick Breads	Apple Fritters	20
Quick Breads	Buttermilk Pancakes	21
Quick Breads	Griddle Cakes	21
Quick Breads	Whole Wheat Pancakes	21
Quick Breads	Apple Pancakes	22
Quick Breads	Sour Cream Coffee Cake	22
Quick Breads	Fruit Platz or Coffee Cake	175
Quick Breads	Molasses Graham Bread	182
Raisins	Fruit Cake	35
Raisins	Christmas Cake	35
Raisins	Old Fashioned Raisin Bars	63
Raisins	7 Cents Pudding	99
Raisins	Dorda Pie	119
Raisins	Raisin Cream Pie	119
Raisins	Green Tomato Mincemeat	121
Raisins	Mincemeat	121
Raisins	Fastnacht Doughnuts	172
Raisins	Rosinen Stritzel	174
Raisins	Homemade Mincemeat	185
Raspberries	Raspberry Dessert	105
Raspberries	Raspberry Vinegar	138
Raspberries	Cranberry-Raspberry Salad	151
Raspberry Jam	Raspberry Squares	59
Remedies	Bread and Milk Poultices	191
Remedies	Simple Ointment	191
Remedies	Homemade Liniment	191
Remedies	Old Fashioned Cough Remedy	191
Remedies	Honey	192
Remedies	Teas and What They are Good For	192
Remedies	Mustard Plaster	192
Remedies	Hair Tonic	193
Remedies	Cider Vinegar	193
Remedies	Lily Whiskey	193
Rhubarb	Rhubarb Tarte	104
Rhubarb	Rhubarb Cake Pudding	105
Rhubarb	Rhubarb Pie with Meringue	115
Rhubarb	Rhubarb-Strawberry Pie	118
Rhubarb	Heavenly Jam	133
Rhubarb	Strawberry Rhubarb Jam	134

Rhubarb	Homemade Rhubarb Juice	142
Rice	Pork Chops and Rice Colonial	91
Rice	Rice Fluff	106
Rice Cereal	Oatmeal Cereal Cookies	47
Rice Flakes	Rice Flake Balls	45
Salad and Salad Dressings	Coleslaw Parfait Salad	152
Salads and Salad Dressings	Sauerkraut Salad	145
Salads and Salad Dressings	Canned Bean Salad	145
Salads and Salad Dressings	Old Fashioned Bean Salad	145
Salads and Salad Dressings	Potato Salad	146
Salads and Salad Dressings	Cabbage Salad	146
Salads and Salad Dressings	Salad of Greens	147
Salads and Salad Dressings	Two Week Cole Slaw	147
Salads and Salad Dressings	Hot Potato Salad	147
Salads and Salad Dressings	Gelatin Salad	148
Salads and Salad Dressings	Orange Gelatin Salad	148
Salads and Salad Dressings	Cranberry Salad	148
Salads and Salad Dressings	California Salad	149
Salads and Salad Dressings	Orange Banana Salad	149
Salads and Salad Dressings	Fruit Cream Dressing	149
Salads and Salad Dressings	Festive Party Salad	150
Salads and Salad Dressings	Tuna Salad	150
Salads and Salad Dressings	Lemon-Lime Gelatin Salad	150
Salads and Salad Dressings	Whipped Cream Topping for Gelatin Salads	151
Salads and Salad Dressings	Vegetable Salad	151
Salads and Salad Dressings	Cranberry- Raspberry Salad	151
Salads and Salad Dressings	Cream Cheese Salad	152
Salads and Salad Dressings	Fruited Cheese Salad	153
Salads and Salad Dressings	Chicken Salad	153
Salads and Salad Dressings	Mexicali Salad Ring	153
Salads and Salad Dressings	Marinated Carrot Salad	154
Salads and Salad Dressings	Horseradish Salad	154
Salads and Salad Dressings	Far East Fruit Plate	155
Salads and Salad Dressings	Quick French Dressing	155
Salads and Salad Dressings	St. Anthony Salad Dressing	155
Salads and Salad Dressings	Hot Mustard	156
Salads and Salad Dressings	Russian Salad Dressing	156
Salads and Salad Dressings	French Dressing	156
Salads and Salad Dressings	Mustard	157
Salads and Salad Dressings	Boiled Salad Dressing	157
Salads and Salad Dressings	Mayonnaise	157
Salads and Salad Dressings	Schmoor Kohl	168
Salads and Salad Dressings	Yellow Bean Salad	183
Salmon	Big Catch Casserole	75
Salmon	Salmon Patties	77
Salmon	Party Buns	81
Sauerkraut	Sauerkraut Cake	31
Sauerkraut	Sauerkraut and Pork	73
Sauerkraut	Sauerkraut Salad	145
Shortbreads	(See Cookies, Squares and Bar Cookies)	
Soap	How to Boil Soap	188
Soups	Cream of Bean Soup	161
Soups	Wiener Potato Soup	161

Soups	Hamburger Soup	162
Soups	Smoked Sausage Potato Soup	162
Soups	Turkey or Chicken Soup	163
Soups	Chinese Soup	163
Soups	Butter Balls or Rivels	163
Soups	Chicken Noodle Soup	163
Soups	Oyster Soup	164
Soups	Bread Soup	164
Soups	Butter Soup	164
Soups	Angel Food Dumplings	164
Soups	Borscht	167
Soups	Potato Soup	188
Special European Mennonite Dishes	Kielke	167
Special European Mennonite Dishes	Piramanie	167
Special European Mennonite Dishes	Fleisch Piroschky	167
Special European Mennonite Dishes	Schmoor Kohl	168
Special European Mennonite Dishes	Bubbat	169
Special European Mennonite Dishes	Apple Moos	169
Special European Mennonite Dishes	Glums Vareneki	169
Special European Mennonite Dishes	Zwetschen Knoedel	170
Special European Mennonite Dishes	Apple Strudel	170
Special European Mennonite Dishes	Christmas Cookies	171
Special European Mennonite Dishes	Nusskuchen	171
Special European Mennonite Dishes	Hungarian Cheesecake	172
Special European Mennonite Dishes	Fastnacht Doughnuts	172
Special European Mennonite Dishes	Rollkuchen	173
Special European Mennonite Dishes	Piroschky	173
Special European Mennonite Dishes	Paska	174
Special European Mennonite Dishes	Rosinen Stritzel	174
Special European Mennonite Dishes	Zwieback	175
Special European Mennonite Dishes 175	Fruit Platz or Coffee	Cake
Special European Mennonite Dishes	Pluskie	176
Special European Mennonite Dishes	Raised Piroschky	176
Special European Mennonite Dishes	Krimmsche Schnittchen	177
Special European Mennonite Dishes	Schnittchen	177
Spinach	Spinach Pie	75
Strawberries	Frozen Berry Fluff	103
Strawberries	Strawberry Pie	114
Strawberries	Relief Sale Strawberry Pie	115
Strawberries	Rhubarb-Strawberry Pie	118
Strawberries	Quantity Fruit Punch	139
Tapioca	Tapioca Fluff	183
Tea Breads	(See Quick Breads)	
Tomatoes	Green Tomato Mincemeat	121
Tomatoes	Fruit and Tomato Relish	127
Tomatoes	Tomato Butter	127
Tomatoes	Tomato Marmalade	133
Tomatoes	Tomato Juice	138
Tongue	Pickled Tongue	89
Tuna	Tuna Noodle Casserole	69
Tuna	Tuna Casserole	70
Tuna	Big Catch Casserole	75

Tuna	Party Buns	81
Tuna	Tuna Salad	150
Turkey	Turkey Pie with English Pastry	70
Turkey	Party Buns	81
Turkey	Leftover Turkey Croquettes	87
Turkey	Turkey Soup	163
Veal	Spanish Veal	90
Walnuts	Hungarian Walnut Strudel	8
Walnuts	Apricot Brazil Bread	11
Walnuts	Applesauce Nut Bread	11
Walnuts	Banana Nut Bread	12
Walnuts	Date Nut Muffins	16
Walnuts	Maple-Nut Chiffon Cake	26
Walnuts	Chocolate Nut Caramels	39
Walnuts	Marmalade Nut Cookies	51
Walnuts	Walnut Logs	52
Walnuts	Fruit Jumbos	53
Walnuts	"O Henry" Squares	59
Walnuts	Butter Nut Chews	61
Walnuts	Maple Walnut Pie	116
Yeast Breads	White Bread	3
Yeast Breads	Whole Wheat Bread	3
Yeast Breads	Rolled Oat Bread	4
Yeast Breads	Basic Sweet Dough	4
Yeast Breads	Swedish Tea Ring	5
Yeast Breads	Cinnamon Rolls	5
Yeast Breads	Jam Ring	5
Yeast Breads	Chelsea Buns	5
Yeast Breads	Cream Buns	6
Yeast Breads	Coffee Cake	6
Yeast Breads	Quick Water Bread	6
Yeast Breads	Oatmeal Rolls	7
Yeast Breads	Refrigerator Rolls	7
Yeast Breads	Plucketts	7
Yeast Breads	Hungarian Walnut Strudel	8
Yeast Breads	Paska	174
Yeast Breads	Rosinen Stritzel	174
Yeast Breads	Zwieback	175
Yeast Breads	Pluskie	176
Yeast Breads	Homemade Bread	184

Order Form

Yes, please send the following:

_____ copies of Treasured Mennonite Recipes - @ 11.95   _____

_____ copies of More Treasured Mennonite Recipes - #2 - @ 11.95   _____
(Available Fall 1993)

(Please add $2.00 per book to a maximum of $4.00)   _____

Total   _____

Please send check or money order to:

In United States send orders to:
Fox Chapel Publishing
Box 7948M
Lancaster, PA 17604-7948

In Canada send orders to:
Blue Ribbon Bookhouse
Box 158
Shakespeare, Ontario
N0B 2P0

Order Form

Yes, please send the following:

_____ copies of Treasured Mennonite Recipes - @ 11.95   _____

_____ copies of More Treasured Mennonite Recipes - #2 - @ 11.95   _____
(Available Fall 1993)

(Please add $2.00 per book to a maximum of $4.00)   _____

Total   _____

Please send check or money order to:

In United States send orders to:
Fox Chapel Publishing
Box 7948M
Lancaster, PA 17604-7948

In Canada send orders to:
Blue Ribbon Bookhouse
Box 158
Shakespeare, Ontario
N0B 2P0

Order Form

Yes, please send the following:

_____ copies of Treasured Mennonite Recipes - @ 11.95 _____

_____ copies of More Treasured Mennonite Recipes - #2 - @ 11.95 _____
(Available Fall 1993)

(Please add $2.00 per book to a maximum of $4.00) _____

Total _____

Please send check or money order to:

In United States send orders to:
Fox Chapel Publishing
Box 7948M
Lancaster, PA 17604-7948

In Canada send orders to:
Blue Ribbon Bookhouse
Box 158
Shakespeare, Ontario
N0B 2P0

Order Form

Yes, please send the following:

_____ copies of Treasured Mennonite Recipes - @ 11.95 _____

_____ copies of More Treasured Mennonite Recipes - #2 - @ 11.95 _____
(Available Fall 1993)

(Please add $2.00 per book to a maximum of $4.00) _____

Total _____

Please send check or money order to:

In United States send orders to:
Fox Chapel Publishing
Box 7948M
Lancaster, PA 17604-7948

In Canada send orders to:
Blue Ribbon Bookhouse
Box 158
Shakespeare, Ontario
N0B 2P0

Order Form

Yes, please send the following:

_____ copies of Treasured Mennonite Recipes - @ 11.95 _____

_____ copies of More Treasured Mennonite Recipes - #2 - @ 11.95 _____
(Available Fall 1993)

(Please add $2.00 per book to a maximum of $4.00) _____

Total _____

Please send check or money order to:

In United States send orders to:
Fox Chapel Publishing
Box 7948M
Lancaster, PA 17604-7948

In Canada send orders to:
Blue Ribbon Bookhouse
Box 158
Shakespeare, Ontario
N0B 2P0

Order Form

Yes, please send the following:

_____ copies of Treasured Mennonite Recipes - @ 11.95 _____

_____ copies of More Treasured Mennonite Recipes - #2 - @ 11.95 _____
(Available Fall 1993)

(Please add $2.00 per book to a maximum of $4.00) _____

Total _____

Please send check or money order to:

In United States send orders to:
Fox Chapel Publishing
Box 7948M
Lancaster, PA 17604-7948

In Canada send orders to:
Blue Ribbon Bookhouse
Box 158
Shakespeare, Ontario
N0B 2P0

Order Form

Yes, please send the following:

_____ copies of Treasured Mennonite Recipes - @ 11.95   _____

_____ copies of More Treasured Mennonite Recipes - #2 - @ 11.95   _____
(Available Fall 1993)

(Please add $2.00 per book to a maximum of $4.00)   _____

Total   _____

Please send check or money order to:

In United States send orders to:
Fox Chapel Publishing
Box 7948M
Lancaster, PA 17604-7948

In Canada send orders to:
Blue Ribbon Bookhouse
Box 158
Shakespeare, Ontario
N0B 2P0

Order Form

Yes, please send the following:

_____ copies of Treasured Mennonite Recipes - @ 11.95   _____

_____ copies of More Treasured Mennonite Recipes - #2 - @ 11.95   _____
(Available Fall 1993)

(Please add $2.00 per book to a maximum of $4.00)   _____

Total   _____

Please send check or money order to:

In United States send orders to:
Fox Chapel Publishing
Box 7948M
Lancaster, PA 17604-7948

In Canada send orders to:
Blue Ribbon Bookhouse
Box 158
Shakespeare, Ontario
N0B 2P0

Metric Conversion Chart

Volume Measurement*

⅛ teaspoon = 0.5 mL
¼ teaspoon = 1 mL
⅓ teaspoon = 1 mL
½ teaspoon = 2 mL
¾ teaspoon = 4 mL
1 teaspoon = 5 mL
½ tablespoon = 7 mL
1 tablespoon = 15 mL
1½ tablespoons = 22 mL
2 tablespoons = 25 mL
3 tablespoons = 45 mL
¼ cup = 50 mL
⅓ cup = 80 mL
½ cup = 125 mL
⅔ cup = 160 mL
¾ cup = 180 mL
1 cup = 250 mL (236.58)
1½ cups = 375 mL
2 cups = 1 pint = 500 mL
2½ cups = 625 mL
3 cups = 750 mL
3½ cups = 825 mL
4 cups = 1 quart = 1 L
1 fluid ounce (2 Tbs.) = 30 mL
4 fluid ounces (½ cup) = 125 mL
8 fluid ounces (1 cup) = 250 mL
12 fluid ounces (1½ cups) = 375 mL
16 fluid ounces (2 cups) = 500 mL
*(including fluid ounces)

Weight (Mass)

½ ounce = 15 g
1 ounce = 30 g (28.35)
2 ounces = 60 g
3 ounces = 85 g
4 ounces = 115 g
8 ounces = 225 g

Baking Pan Sizes

Utensil	Metric Volume	Metric Measure in cm	Closest Size in inches or Volume
Baking or	2 L	20x5	8x2
Cake Pan	2.5 L	22x5	9x2
	3 L	30x20x5	12x8x2
	3.5 L	33x23x5	13x9x2
Loaf Pan	1.5 L	20x10x7	8x4x3
	2 L	23x13x7	9x5x3
Round Layer	1.2 L	20x4	8x1½
Cake Pan	1.5 L	23x4	9x1½
Pie Pan	750 mL	20x3	8x1¼
	1 L	23x3	9x1¼
Baking Dish	1 L		1 quart
or Casserole	1.5 L		1½ quart
	2 K		2 qt.

12 ounces = 340 g
16 ounces = 1 pound = 450 g
2 pounds = 900 g

1½ inches = 4 cm
2 inches = 5 cm

Oven Temperatures*

250° F = 120° C
275° F = 140° C
300° F = 150° C
325° F = 160° C
350° F = 180° C
375° F = 190° C
400° F = 200° C
425° F = 220° C
450° F = 230° C
*(- 32 x 5 ÷9)(low temps.—
do exact conversion)

Dimensions

1/16 inch = 2 mm
⅛ inch = 0.5 cm
3/16 inch = 0.5 cm
¼ inch = 0.5 cm
⅜ inch = 1 cm
½ inch = 1.5 cm
⅝ inch = 1.5 cm
¾ inch = 2 cm
1 inch = 2.5 cm (2.54)